Small Business Made Simple

Small Business
Legal Forms
Simplified

Small Business Legal Forms Simplified

by Daniel Sitarz
Attorney-at-Law

Nova Publishing Company
Small Business and Consumer Legal Books and Software
Carbondale, Illinois

Editorial and research assistance by Janet Harris Sitarz, L̶̶̶̶̶̶̶̶̶̶̶̶ and Melanie Bray. Cover and interior design by Linda Jorgensen-B̶̶̶̶̶̶̶̶̶. M̶̶̶̶̶̶̶̶̶̶̶̶ ed States.

ISBN 0-935755-98-5   Book w/CD   ($29.95)
Library of Congress Catalog Card Number 91-4130

Library of Congress Cataloging-in-Publication Data
    Sitarz, Dan, 1948-
        Small Business Legal Forms Simplified / Daniel Sitarz
        Formerly titled: *The Complete Book of Small Business Legal Forms*
        P. cm-(Small business made simple)
        ISBN 0-935755-98-5
        1. Small business—Law and legislation—United States—Forms. 2. Forms (Law)—
    United States—Popular works.
    I. Title. II. Series
    KF 1659.A65S43 2004   346.73'0652'0269--dc20 [347.3066520269]

Nova Publishing Company is dedicated to providing up-to-date and accurate legal information to the public. All Nova publications are periodically revised to contain the latest available legal information.

4th Edition; 1st Printing:	January, 2005		1st Edition; 4th Printing:	August, 1994
3rd Edition; 2nd Printing:	October, 2001		1st Edition; 3rd Printing:	May, 1992
3rd Edition; 1st Printing:	December, 2000		1st Edition; 2nd Printing:	October, 1991
2nd Edition; 2nd Printing:	April, 1998		1st Edition; 1st Printing	August, 1991
2nd Edition; 1st Printing:	September, 1996			

This publication is designed to provide accurate and authoritative information in regard to the subject matter covered. It is sold with the understanding that the publisher and author are not engaged in rendering legal, accounting, or other professional services. If legal advice or other expert assistance is required, the services of a competent professional person should be sought.
—*From a Declaration of Principles jointly adopted by a Committee of the American Bar Association and a Committee of Publishers*

DISCLAIMER

Because of possible unanticipated changes in governing statutes and case law relating to the application of any information contained in this book, the author, publisher, and any and all persons or entities involved in any way in the preparation, publication, sale, or distribution of this book disclaim all responsibility for the legal effects or consequences of any document prepared or action taken in reliance upon information contained in this book. No representations, either express or implied, are made or given regarding the legal consequences of the use of any information contained in this book. Purchasers and persons intending to use this book for the preparation of any legal documents are advised to check specifically on the current applicable laws in any jurisdiction in which they intend the documents to be effective.

Nova Publishing Company
Small Business and Consumer Legal Books and Software
1103 West College St.
Carbondale, IL 62901
Editorial: (800) 748-1175

Distributed by:
National Book Network
4501 Forbes Blvd., Suite 200
Lanham, MD 20706
Orders: (800) 462-6420

Nova Publishing Company Green Business Policies

Nova Publishing Company is committed to preserving ancient forests and natural resources. Our company's policy is to print all of our books on recycled paper, with no less than 30% post-consumer waste de-inked in a chlorine-free process. In addition, all Nova books are printed usng soy-based inks. As a result, for the printing of this book, we have saved:

32.7 trees • 9,450 gallons of water • 5,535 kilowatt hours of electricity • 81 pounds of pollution

Nova Publishing Company is a member of Green Press Initiative, a nonprofit program dedicated to supporting publishers in their efforts to reduce their use of fiber obtained from endangered forests. For more information, go to www.greenpressinitiative.org. In addition, Nova uses all compact fluorescent lighting; recycles all office paper products, aluminum and plastic beverage containers, and printer cartridges; uses 100% post-consumer fiber, process-chlorine-free, acid-free paper for 95% of in-house paper use; and, when possible, uses electronic equipment that is EPA Energy Star-certified. Finally, all carbon emissions from office energy use are offset by the purchase of wind-energy credits that are used to subsidize the building of wind turbines on the Rosebud Sioux Reservation in South Dakota (see www.nativeenergy.com/coop).

Table of Contents

List of Forms-on-CD

Business Operation Agreements

Agreement for Sale of Business
Agreement for Sale of Business Assets
Agreement Not to Compete
Affidavit of Use of Fictitious Business Name
Notice of Intention to Use Fictitious Name
Partnership Agreement

Contracts

Contract
Extension of Contract
Modification of Contract
Termination of Contract
Assignment of Contract
Consent to Assignment of Contract
Notice of Assignment of Contract
Notice of Breach of Contract

Signatures and Notary Acknowledgments

Corporate Acknowledgment
Corporate Signature Line
Partnership Acknowledgment
Partnership Signature Line
Limited Liability Company Acknowledgment
Limited Liability Company Signature Line
Sole Proprietorship Acknowledgment
Sole Proprietorship Signature Line
Power of Attorney Acknowledgment
Power of Attorney Signature Line
Individual Acknowledgment
Individual Signature Line
Husband and Wife Acknowledgment
Husband and Wife Signature Line

Powers of Attorney

Unlimited Power of Attorney
Limited Power of Attorney
Durable Unlimited Power of Attorney
Durable Limited Power of Attorney
Revocation of Power of Attorney

Releases

General Release
Mutual Release
Specific Release
Release of Mechanic's Liens

Receipts

Receipt in Full
Receipt on Account
Receipt for Goods

Leases of Real Estate

Residential Lease
Commercial Lease
Assignment of Lease
Consent to Assignment of Lease
Notice of Assignment of Lease
Amendment of Lease
Extension of Lease
Sublease
Consent to Sublease of Lease
Notice of Breach of Lease
Notice of Rent Default
Notice to Vacate Property
Landlord's Notice to Terminate Lease
Tenant's Notice to Terminate Lease
Mutual Termination of Lease
Receipt for Lease Security Deposit
Rent Receipt
Notice of Lease

Rental of Personal Property

Personal Property Rental Agreement (Simple)
Personal Property Rental Agreement (Complex)
Renter's Notice to Terminate Rental Agreement
Owner's Notice to Terminate Rental Agreement

Sale of Personal Property

Contract for Sale of Personal Property
Bill of Sale, with Warranties
Bill of Sale, without Warranties
Bill of Sale, Subject to Debt

Sale of Real Estate

Agreement to Sell Real Estate
Option to Buy Real Estate Agreement
Quitclaim Deed
Warranty Deed
Affidavit of Title
Deed of Trust
Mortgage

Employment Documents

General Employment Contract
Employee Confidentiality Agreement
Employee Patents and Inventions Agreement
Consent to Release Employment Information
Independent Contractor Agreement
Contractor/Subcontractor Agreement

Business Credit Documents

Business Credit Application
Notice of Approval of Business Credit Application
Request for Bank Credit Reference
Request for Trade Credit Reference
Request for Credit Information

Business Financing Documents

Security Agreement
Receipt for Collateral
General Guaranty
Release of Security Interest
U.C.C. Financing Statement
Release of U.C.C. Financing Statement

Promissory Notes

Promissory Note (Installment Repayment)
Promissory Note (Lump Sum Repayment)
Promissory Note (on Demand)
Promissory Note (Secured)
Promissory Note (with Guarantor)
Release of Promissory Note
Demand and Notice of Default on Installment Promissory Note
Demand and Notice for Full Payment on Installment Promissory Note
Demand and Notice for Payment on Demand Promissory Note
Demand and Notice for Payment from Guarantor on Demand Promissory Note

Purchase of Goods Documents

Request for Price Quote
Notice of Acceptance of Order
Notice of Conditional Acceptance of Non-Conforming Goods
Notice of Rejection of Non-Conforming Goods
Notice of Conditional Acceptance of Defective Goods
Notice of Rejection of Defective Goods
Notice of Rejection of Order
Notice of Refusal to Accept Delivery
Notice of Demand for Delivery of Goods
Notice of Cancellation of Purchase Order
Notice of Return of Goods Sold on Approval

Sale of Goods Documents

Demand for Explanation of Rejected Goods
Notice of Replacement of Rejected Goods
Notice of Goods Sold on Approval
Contract for Sale of Goods
Contract for Sale of Goods on Consignment
Bulk Transfer Affidavit
Bulk Transfer Notice

Collection Documents

Request for Payment
Second Request for Payment
Final Demand for Payment
Assignment of Account for Collection
Notice of Assignment of Account for Collection
Appointment of Collection Agent
Notice of Appointment of Collection Agent
Notice of Disputed Account
Offer to Settle Disputed Account
Agreement to Settle Disputed Account
Notice of Dishonored Check
Stop Payment on Check Order

Miscellaneous Business Documents

Affidavit
Indemnity Agreement
Waiver and Assumption of Risk
Contract Exhibit
Assignment and Transfer of Copyright
Request for Reprint Permission

Reprint Permission
Model's Photographic Release

Forms-on-CD (*Not included in book*)

Federal Lead Brochure: "Protect Your Family from Lead in Your Home"
Glossary

Instructions for Using Forms-on-CD

Quick-Start Installation for PCs

1   Insert the enclosed CD in your computer.
2. The installation program will start automatically. Follow the onscreen dialogue and make your appropriate choices.
3   If the CD installation does not start automatically, click on START, then RUN, then BROWSE, and select your CD drive, and then select the file "Install.exe." Finally, click OK to run the installation program.
4. Open the "Readme.doc" document (which should be visible on your Windows desktop). Print out and follow instructions on the "Readme.doc" document.

Installation Instructions for MACs

1. Insert the enclosed CD in your computer.
2. Copy the folder "Forms for Macs" to your hard drive.
3. Open the folder and print out the "readme.doc" file.
4. Double-click on the file "acrobat reader installation.exe." This will install the Adobe Acrobat Reader program.
5. Follow the instructions on the Readme document.

Preface

This book is part of Nova Publishing Company's continuing series on *Small Business Made Simple*. The various self-help legal guides in this series are prepared by licensed attorneys who feel that public access to the American legal system is long overdue.

Law in American society is far more pervasive than ever before. There are legal consequences to virtually every public and most private actions in today's world. Leaving knowledge of the law within the hands of only the lawyers in such a society is not only foolish, but dangerous as well. A free society depends, in large part, on an informed citizenry. This book and others in Nova's *Small Business Made Simple* series are intended to provide the necessary information to those members of the public who wish to use and understand the law for themselves.

However, in an area as complex as business law, encompassing topics as diverse as the Uniform Commercial Code, property law, constitutional law, and legal contracts, it is not always prudent to attempt to handle every legal situation which arises without the aid of a competent attorney. Although the information presented in this book will give its readers a basic understanding of the areas of law covered, it is not intended that this text entirely substitute for experienced legal assistance in all situations. Throughout this book there are references to those particular situations in which the aid of a lawyer is strongly recommended.

Regardless of whether or not a lawyer is ultimately retained in certain situations, the legal information in this handbook will enable the reader to understand the framework of business law in this country and how to effectively use legal forms in the operation of their small business.

To try and make that task as easy as possible, technical legal jargon has been eliminated whenever possible and plain English used instead. Naturally, plain and easily understood English is not only perfectly proper for use in all legal documents but, in most cases, leads to far less confusion on the part of later readers. When it is necessary in this book to use a legal term which may be unfamiliar to most people, the word will be shown in *italics* and defined when first used.

CHAPTER 1
Using Legal Forms in Your Business

The business arena in America operates on a daily assortment of legal forms. There are more legal forms in use in American business than are used in the operations and government of many foreign countries. The small business is not immune to this flood of legal forms. The legal system in America has a profound impact on the operation of every business, from the giant multinational corporation to the tiny one-person enterprise. While large corporations are able to obtain and pay expensive lawyers to deal with their legal problems and paperwork, most small businesses cannot afford such a course of action. Whether it is in the form of signing a lease for office space, obtaining a contract for work, or accepting a shipment of goods, the small businessperson must deal with a variety of legal documents nearly every business day, usually without the aid of an attorney. Unfortunately, many business people who are confronted with such forms do not understand the legal ramifications of the use of these forms. They simply sign the lease, contract, or bill of sale with the expectation that it is a fairly standard document without any unusual legal provisions. They trust that the details of the particular document will fall within what is generally accepted within the industry or trade. In most cases, this may be true. In many situations, however, it is not. Our court system is clogged with cases in which two businesses are battling over what was really intended by the incomprehensible legal language in a certain contract.

Much of the confusion over business legal contracts comes from two areas. First, there is a general lack of understanding among many in business regarding the framework of contract law. Second, many contracts are written in antiquated legal jargon that is difficult for most lawyers to understand and nearly impossible for a layperson to comprehend. Although this book will provide an overview of the uses of legal contracts in many standard situations, it is not intended to be a complete reference on the subject of contract law.

The contracts and various legal documents that are used in this book are, however, written in plain English. Standard legal jargon, as used in most lawyer-prepared documents, is, for most people, totally incomprehensible. Despite the lofty arguments by attorneys regarding the need for such strained and difficult language, the vast majority of legalese is absolutely unnecessary. Clarity, simplicity, and readability should be the goal in legal documents. In most business contexts, "buyer" and "seller," "landlord" and "tenant," or some other straightforward term of definition of the parties involved is possible.

Unfortunately, certain obscure legal terms are the only words that accurately and precisely describe some things in certain legal contexts. In those few cases, the unfamiliar legal term will be defined when first used. Generally, however, simple terms are used.

All of the legal documents contained in this book have been prepared in essentially the same manner that attorneys create legal forms. Many people believe that lawyers prepare each legal document that they compose entirely from scratch. Nothing could be further from the truth. Invariably, lawyers begin their preparation of a legal document with a standardized legal form book. Every law library has multi-volume sets of these encyclopedic texts which contain blank forms for virtually every conceivable legal situation. Armed with these pre-prepared legal forms, lawyers, in many cases, simply fill in the blanks and have their secretaries retype the form for the client. Of course, the client is generally unaware of this process.

This book provides the small businessperson with a set of legal forms that has been prepared with the problems and normal transactions of the entrepreneur in mind. These forms are intended to be used in those situations that are clearly described by their terms. Of course, while most business transactions will fall within the bounds of standard business practices, some legal circumstances will present non-standard situations. The forms in this book are designed to be readily adaptable to most usual business situations. They may be carefully altered to conform to the particular transaction that confronts your business. However, if you are faced with a complex or tangled business situation, the advice of a competent lawyer is recommended. If you wish, you may also create forms for certain standard legal transactions for your business and have your lawyer check them for any local legal circumstances.

The proper and cautious use of the forms provided in this book will allow the typical small businessperson to save considerable money on legal costs over the course of the life of the business, while enabling the business to comply with legal and governmental regulations. Perhaps more important, these forms will provide a method by which the businessperson can avoid costly misunderstandings about what exactly was intended in a particular situation or transaction. By using the forms provided to clearly set out the terms and conditions of everyday business dealings, disputes over what was really meant can be avoided. This protection will allow the business to avoid many potential lawsuits and operate more efficiently in compliance with the law.

How to Use This Book

In each chapter of this book you will find an introductory section that will give you an overview of the types of situations in which the forms in that chapter will generally be used. Following that overview, there will be a brief explanation of the specific uses for each form. Included in the information provided for each form will be a discussion of the legal terms and conditions provided in the form. Finally, for each form, there is a listing of the information that must be compiled to complete the form.

The preferable manner for using these forms is to use the enclosed Forms-on-CD. Please refer to the readme.doc file on the Forms-on-CD for specific instructions on completing the computer-ready forms. However, it is perfectly acceptable to prepare these forms directly from the book by making a copy of the form, filling in the information that is necessary, and then retyping the form in its entirety on clean white letter-sized paper.

For purposes of simplification, most of the forms in this book are set out in a form as would be used by two individuals. However, any of the various forms can be adapted for use between two business entities or an individual and a business entity. Please use the appropriate signature lines from Chapter 4 if you wish to modify the basic form as it is set forth. If businesses are parties to the contract, please identify the name and type of business entity (for example: Jackson Car Stereo, a New York sole proprietorship, etc.) in the first section of the contract. If notary acknowledgments are required for a particular form, please also refer to Chapter 4 for the correct acknowledgment form to use.

Please also note that any forms which begin with "NOTICE" should be sent to the person or company receiving the form by certified mail. This may be a requirement under various laws, including the Uniform Commercial Code.

Many of the forms in this book have blanks for inserting the state or county. If you are a resident of Louisiana, substitute "parish" for "county." If you are a resident of Pennsylvania, Massachusetts, Virginia, or Kentucky, substitute "Commonwealth" for "state." If you are a resident of Washington D.C., please substitute "District of Columbia" for "state."

In most cases, masculine and feminine terms have been eliminated and the generic "it" or "them" used instead. In the few situations in which this leads to awkward sentence construction, "his or her" or "he or she" may be used instead.

It is recommended that you review the table of contents of this book in order to gain a broad overview of the range and type of legal documents that are available. Then, before you prepare any of the forms for use, you should carefully read the introductory information and instructions in the chapter where the particular form is contained. Try to be as detailed and specific as possible as you fill in these forms. The more precise the description, the less likelihood that later disputes may develop over what was actually intended by the language chosen. The careful preparation and use of the legal forms in this book should provide the typical small business with most of the legal documents necessary for day-to-day operations. If in doubt as to whether a particular form will work in a specific application, please consult a competent lawyer.

CHAPTER 2
Business Operation Agreements

One of the first decisions that a potential business owner must confront is how the business should be structured and operated. This crucial decision must be made even before the business has actually begun operations. The legal documents which will generally accompany the formation of a business can follow many different patterns, depending on the particular situation and the type of business to be undertaken. There are two initial decisions which must be made in order to begin a business operation: the type of business entity to be used and from where the business assets will come.

First, the type of business entity to be used must be selected. There are many basic forms of business operating entities. The five most common forms are:

- Sole proprietorship
- Partnership
- Corporation
- S-corporation
- Limited liability company

The choice of entity for a particular business depends on many factors. Which of these forms of business organization is chosen can have a great impact on the success of the business. The structure chosen will have an effect on how easy it is to obtain financing, how taxes are paid, how accounting records are kept, whether personal assets are at risk in the venture, the amount of control the "owner" has over the business, and many other aspects of the business.

Keep in mind that the initial choice of business organization need not be the final choice. It is often wise to begin with the most simple form, the sole proprietorship, until the business progresses to a point where another form is clearly indicated. This allows the business to begin in the least complicated manner and allows the owner to retain total control in the important formative period of the business. As the business grows and the potential for liability and tax burdens increase, circumstances may dictate a re-examination of the business structure. The advantages and disadvantages of the five choices of business operation are detailed on the following pages.

Sole Proprietorship

A sole proprietorship is both the simplest and the most prevalent form of business organization. An important reason for this is that it is the least regulated of all types of business structures. Technically, the *sole proprietorship* is the traditional unincorporated one-person business. For legal and tax purposes, the business is the owner. It has no existence outside the owner. The liabilities of the business are personal to the owner and the business ends when the owner dies. On the other hand, all of the profits are also personal to the owner and the sole owner has full control of the business. For more information on sole proprietorships, please see Nova Publishing Company's *Sole Proprietorship: Small Business Start-Up Kit*, by Dan Sitarz.

Disadvantages

Perhaps the most important factor to consider before choosing this type of business structure is that all of the personal and business assets of the sole owner are at risk in the sole proprietorship. If the demands of the creditors of the business exceed those assets which were formally placed in the name of the business, the creditors may reach the personal assets of the owner of the sole proprietorship. Legal judgments for damages arising from the operation of the business may also be enforced against the owner's personal assets. This unlimited liability is probably the greatest drawback to this type of business form. Of course, insurance coverage of various types can lessen the dangers inherent in having one's personal assets at risk in a business. However, as liability insurance premiums continue to skyrocket, it is unlikely that a fledgling small business can afford to insure against all manner of contingencies and at the maximum coverage levels necessary to guard against all risk to personal assets.

A second major disadvantage to the sole proprietorship as a form of business structure is the potential difficulty in obtaining business loans. Often, in starting a small business, there is insufficient collateral to obtain a loan and the sole owner must mortgage her or his own house or other personal assets to obtain the loan. This, of course, puts the sole proprietor's personal assets in a direct position of risk should the business fail. Banks and other lending institutions are often reluctant to loan money for initial small business start-ups due to the high risk of failure for small businesses. Without a proven track record, it is quite difficult for a small business owner to adequately present a loan proposal based on a sufficiently stable cash flow to satisfy most banks.

A further disadvantage to a sole proprietorship is the lack of continuity which is inherent in the business form. If the owner dies, the business ceases to exist. Of course, the assets and liabilities of the business will pass to the heirs of the owner, but the expertise and knowledge of how the business was successfully carried on will often die with the owner. Small sole proprietorships are seldom carried on profitably after the death of the owner.

Advantages

The advantage of the sole proprietorship as a business structure which appeals to most people is the total control the owner has over the business. Subject only to economic considerations and certain legal restrictions, there is total freedom to operate the business however one chooses. Many people feel that this factor alone is enough to overcome the inherent disadvantages in this form of business.

Related to this is the simplicity of organization of the sole proprietorship. Other than maintenance of sufficient records for tax purposes, there are no legal requirements on how the business is operated. Of course, the prudent businessperson will keep adequate records and sufficiently organize the business for its most efficient operation. But there are no outside forces dictating how such internal decisions are made in the sole proprietorship. The sole owner makes all decisions in this type of business. As was mentioned earlier, the sole proprietorship is the least regulated of all businesses. Normally, the only license necessary is a local business license, usually obtained by simply paying a fee to a local registration authority. In addition, it may be necessary to file an affidavit with local authorities and publish a notice in a local newspaper if the business is operated under an assumed or fictitious name. This is necessary to allow creditors to have access to the actual identity of the true owner of the business, since it is the owner who will be personally liable for the debts and obligations of the business. The forms necessary for this are included in this chapter.

Finally, it may be necessary to register with local, state, and federal tax bodies for I.D. numbers and for the purpose of collection of sales and other taxes. Contact your local and state taxing authorities for information on registration and tax liabilities for sole proprietorships. Other than these few simple registrations, from a legal standpoint little else is required to start up a business as a sole proprietorship.

The final and important advantages to the sole proprietorship are the various tax benefits available to an individual. The losses or profits of the sole proprietorship are considered personal to the owner. The losses are directly deductible against any other income the owner may have and the profits are taxed only once at the marginal rate of the owner. In many instances, this may have distinct advantages over the method by which partnerships are taxed or the double taxation of corporations, particularly in the early stages of the business.

Partnership

A *partnership* is a relationship existing between two or more persons who join together to carry on a trade or business. Each partner contributes money, property, labor, or skill to the partnership and, in return, expects to share in the profits or losses of the business. A partnership is usually based on a partnership agreement of some type, although the agreement need not be a formal document. It may simply be an oral understanding between the partners, although this is not recommended.

A simple joint undertaking to share expenses is not considered a partnership, nor is a mere co-ownership of property that is maintained and leased or rented. To be considered a partnership for legal and tax purposes, the following factors are usually considered:

- The partner's conduct in carrying out the provisions of the partnership agreement
- The relationship of the parties
- The abilities and contributions of each party to the partnership
- The control each partner has over the partnership income and the purposes for which the income is used

For more detailed information, please see Nova Publishing Company's *Partnership: Small Business Start-Up Kit*, by Dan Sitarz.

Disadvantages

The disadvantages to the partnership form of business begin with the potential for conflict between the partners. Of all forms of business organization, the partnership has spawned more disagreements than any other. This is generally traceable to the lack of a decisive initial partnership agreement which clearly outlines the rights and duties of the partners. This disadvantage can be partially overcome with a comprehensive partnership agreement. However, there is still the seemingly inherent difficulty that many people have in working within the framework of a partnership, regardless of the initial agreement between the partners.

A further disadvantage to the partnership structure is that each partner is subject to unlimited personal liability for the debts of the partnership. The potential liability in a partnership is even greater than that encountered in a sole proprietorship. This is due to the fact that in a partnership the personal risk for which one may be liable is partially out of one's direct control and may be accrued due to actions on the part of another person. Each partner is liable for all of the debts of the partnership, regardless of which of the partners may have been responsible for their accumulation.

Related to the business risks of personal financial liability is the potential personal legal liability for the negligence of another partner. In addition, each partner may even be liable for the negligence of an employee of the partnership if such negligence takes place during the usual course of business of the partnership. Again, the attendant risks are broadened by the potential for liability based on the acts of other persons. Of course, general liability insurance can counteract this drawback to some extent to protect the personal and partnership assets of each partner.

Again, as with the sole proprietorship, the partnership lacks the advantage of continuity. A partnership is usually automatically terminated upon the death of any partner. A final accounting and a division of assets and liabilities is generally necessary in such an instance unless specific methods under which the partnership may be continued have been outlined in the partnership agreement.

Finally, certain benefits of corporate organization are not available to a partnership. Since a partnership cannot obtain financing through public stock offerings, large infusions of capital are more difficult for a partnership to raise than for a corporation. In addition, many of the fringe-benefit programs that are available to corporations (such as certain pension and profit-sharing arrangements) are not available to partnerships.

Advantages

A partnership, by virtue of combining the credit potential of the various partners, has an inherently greater opportunity for business credit than is generally available to a sole proprietorship. In addition, the assets that are placed in the name of the partnership may often be used directly as collateral for business loans. The pooling of the personal capital of the partners generally provides the partnership with an advantage over the sole proprietorship in the area of cash availability. However, as noted above, the partnership does not have as great a potential for financing as does a corporation.

As with the sole proprietorship, there may be certain tax advantages to operation of a business as a partnership, as opposed to a corporation. The profits generated by a partnership may be distributed directly to the partners without incurring any "double" tax liability, as is the case with the distribution of corporate profits in the form of dividends to the shareholders. Income from a partnership is taxed at personal income tax rates. Note, however, that depending on the individual tax situation of each partner, this aspect could prove to be a disadvantage.

For a business in which two or more people desire to share in the work and in the profits, a partnership is often the structure chosen. It is, potentially, a much simpler form of business organization than the corporate form. Less start-up costs are necessary and there is limited regulation of partnerships. However, the simplicity of this form of business can be deceiving. A sole proprietor knows that his or her actions will determine how the business will prosper and that he or she is, ultimately, personally responsible for the success or failure of the enterprise. In a partnership, however, the duties, obligations, and commitments of each partner are often ill-defined. This lack of definition of the status of each partner can lead to serious difficulties and disagreements.

In order to clarify the rights and responsibilities of each partner and be certain of the tax status of the partnership, it is good business procedure to have a written partnership agreement. All states have adopted a version of the Uniform Partnership Act. Although state law will supply the general boundaries of partnerships and even specific partnership agreement terms if they are not addressed by a written partnership agreement, it is more conducive to a clear understanding of the business structure if the partner's agreements are put in writing. The following matters need to be considered for inclusion in the agreement:

- The amount and type of cash, services, or property to be contributed by each partner
- The division of profits and losses of the partnership
- Provisions for keeping accurate books and records
- Provision for the management of the partnership
- Methods for termination and dissolution of the partnership

Corporation

A *corporation* is a creation of law. It is governed by the laws of the state of incorporation and the state or states in which it does business. In recent years it has become the business structure of choice for many small businesses. Corporations are, generally, a more complex form of business operation than either a sole proprietorship or partnership. They are also subject to far more state regulations regarding both their formation and operation. Because of this, legal documents for the formation of a corporation are beyond the scope of this book and are not included. Legal forms for the formation and operation of a corporation are contained in Nova Publishing's *Incorporate Now!*, by Dan Sitarz. The following discussion is provided in order to allow the potential business owner an understanding of this type of business operation.

The corporation is an artificial entity. It is created by filing Articles of Incorporation with the proper state authorities. This gives the corporation its legal existence and the right to carry on business. Adoption of *corporate bylaws*, or internal rules of operation, is often the first business of the corporation. In its simplest form, the corporate organizational structure consists of the following levels:

- **Shareholders:** who own shares of the business but do not contribute to the direct management of the corporation, other than by electing the directors of the corporation

- **Directors:** who may be shareholders, but as directors do not own any of the business. They are responsible, jointly as members of the board of directors of the corporation, for making the major business decisions of the corporation, including appointing the officers of the corporation

- **Officers:** who may be shareholders and/or directors, but, as officers, do not own any of the business. The officers (generally the president, vice president, secretary, and treasurer) are responsible for the day-to-day operation of the business

Disadvantages

Due to the nature of the organizational structure in a corporation, a certain degree of individual control is necessarily lost by incorporation. The officers, as appointees of the board of directors, are answerable to the board for management decisions. The board of directors, on the other hand, is not entirely free from restraint, since they are responsible to the shareholders for prudent business management of the corporation.

The technical formalities of corporation formation and operation must be strictly observed in order for a business to reap the benefits of corporate existence. For this reason, there is an additional burden and expense to the corporation of detailed recordkeeping that is seldom present in other forms of business organization. Corporate decisions are, in general, more complicated due to the various levels of control and all such decisions must be carefully documented. Corporate meetings, both at the shareholder and director levels, are more formal and more frequent. In addition, the actual formation of the corporation is more expensive than the formation of either a sole proprietorship or partnership. Finally, corporations are subject to a greater level of governmental regulation than any other type of business entity. These complications have the potential to overburden a small business struggling to survive.

Finally, the profits of a corporation, when distributed to the shareholders in the form of dividends, are subject to being taxed twice. The first tax comes at the corporate level. The distribution of any corporate profits to the investors in the form of dividends is not a deductible business expense for the corporation. Thus, any dividends that are distributed to shareholders have already been subject to corporate income tax. The second level of tax is imposed at the personal level. The receipt of corporate dividends is considered income to the individual shareholder and is taxed as such. This potential for higher taxes due to a corporate business structure can be moderated by many factors, however.

Advantages

One of the most important advantages to the corporate form of business structure is the potential limited liability of the founders of the corporation and investors in the corporation. The liability for corporate debts is limited, in general, to the amount of money each owner has contributed to the corporation. Unless the corporation is essentially a shell for a one-person business or the corporation is grossly undercapitalized or under-insured, the personal assets of the owners are not at risk if the corporation fails. The shareholders stand to lose only what they invested. This factor is very important in attracting investors as the business grows.

A corporation can have a *perpetual* existence. Theoretically, a corporation can last forever. This may be a great advantage if there are potential future changes in ownership of the business in the offing. Changes that would cause a partnership to be dissolved or terminated often will not affect the corporation. This continuity can be an important factor in establishing a stable business image and a permanent relationship with others in the industry.

Unlike a partnership, in which no one may become a partner without the consent of the other partners, shareholders of corporate stock can freely sell, trade, or give away their stock unless formally restricted by reasonable corporate decisions. The new owner of such stock is then a new owner of the business in the proportionate share of stock obtained. This freedom offers potential investors a liquidity to shift assets that is not present in the partnership form of business. The sale of shares by the corporation is also an attractive method by which to raise needed capital. The sale of shares of a corporation, however, is subject to many governmental regulations, on both the state and federal levels.

Taxation is listed both as an advantage and as a disadvantage for the corporation. Depending on many factors, the use of a corporation can increase or decrease the actual income tax paid in operating a corporate business. In addition, corporations may set aside surplus earnings (up to certain levels) without any negative tax consequences. Finally, corporations are able to offer a much greater variety of fringe-benefit programs to employees and officers than any other type of business entity. Various retirement, stock-option, and profit-sharing plans are only open to corporate participation.

S-Corporation

The *S-corporation* is a certain type of corporation that is available for specific tax purposes. It is a creature of the Internal Revenue Service. Its purpose is to allow small corporations to choose to be taxed like a partnership, but to also enjoy many of the benefits of a corporation. Formation of an S-corporation is beyond the scope of this book. Legal forms for the formation and operation of an S-corporation are contained in Nova Publishing's *S-Corporation: The Small Business Start-Up Kit*, by Dan Sitarz. The following discussion is provided in order to allow the potential business owner an understanding of this type of business operation.

In general, to qualify as an S-corporation under current IRS rules, a corporation must have no more than 75 shareholders, all of whom must be individuals; it must only have one class of stock; and each of the shareholders must consent to the choice of S-corporation status.

The S-corporation retains all of the advantages and disadvantages of the traditional corporation except in the area of taxation. For tax purposes, S-corporation shareholders are treated similarly to partners in a partnership. The income, losses, and deductions generated by an S-corporation are "passed through" the corporate entity to the individual shareholders. Thus, there is no "double" taxation of an S-type corporation. In addition, unlike a standard corporation, shareholders of S-corporations can deduct personally any corporate losses.

Limited Liability Company

A relatively new business form is the *limited liability company*. This business form has been adopted in some manner in all states. It is, essentially, a non-incorporated business form which has been given limited legal liability by legislative mandate. Thus, this hybrid type of business has the pass-through taxation advantages of a partnership and the limited legal liability of a corporation. This type of company consists of one or more members/owners who manage the company. There may also be non-member managers employed to handle the business. As a hybrid-type business structure, this form has many of the same advantages and disadvantages as both corporations (particulary S-corporations) and partnerships. One unique advantage that the limited liability company has over standard corporations is the increased flexibility to allocate profits and losses to its members. As this is a new form of business, you are advised to consult a competent business lawyer for assistance in operating as a limited liability company or check out Nova Publishing Company's *Limited Liability Company: Small Business Start-up Kit*, by Dan Sitarz.

Instructions

In addition to selecting the type of structure that the business will take, the other important factor in the initial start-up of a business is where the basic assets of the business will come from. From the point of view of someone who is starting a business, the equipment and supplies needed to begin a business are often purchased from an on-going concern. A purchase of business assets for the purpose of beginning an enterprise will generally take two forms: the purchase of an entire business or the purchase of specific assets and equipment only. There are two legal agreements included in this chapter for these situations. Their use is outlined below.

The following documents are included in this chapter for use in purchasing, selling, or forming a business:

Agreement for Sale of Business: This form should be used when one party is purchasing an entire business from another party. The form, as shown in this book, is set up for use in the sale of a sole proprietorship to an individual. This structure can be easily adapted to fit other particular situations if necessary. For example, if the business being sold is a partnership and the buyer is a corporation, a few simple substitutions will be necessary to change the document to the appropriate form. Simply substitute the name and address of the partnership for the seller's name wherever indicated and substitute the name and address of the corporate buyer where necessary. If changes are made in the type of entity doing the buying or selling on this form, the appropriate notarization and signature line from Chapter 4 must be used also. *Note:* The notarization on this form is only necessary if the sale of the business includes the sale of real estate. A notarization will be needed in order to record this document with the appropriate county office.

The following information will have to be used to fill in this form:

- Name and address of the seller
- Name and address of the buyer
- Type, name, and address of business being sold
- A complete list of the business assets being sold
- The total amount being paid for the business
- How this total amount is allocated among the assets being sold
- How the total amount will be paid
  - The amount of earnest money
  - The amount of downpayment paid at closing
  - The amount of a promissory note
    - The interest rate of the note
    - The term of the note
    - The amount of monthly payments of the note
- The closing date of the sale
- The location of the closing of the sale
- The documents of sale that the seller will provide at closing
- Any adjustments to the sale price that must be made at closing
- An accounting balance sheet of the business
- The terms of an agreement not to compete with the buyer

- How long such an agreement will last
- The geographical area covered by the agreement
- The amount of insurance the buyer agrees to carry on the business
- Any additional terms of agreement the parties wish to include
- The name of the state whose laws will govern the agreement

The sale of a complete and ongoing business is one of the most complex business transactions that a small businessperson will encounter. It may incorporate many of the legal documents that are contained in this book. Be very careful as you prepare this document to coordinate it with all of the necessary other documents. Note that you may also need to use the following additional documents in conjunction with the basic Agreement for Sale of Business form:

- Exhibit A and/or B (Contract Exhibit form from Chapter 19)
- U.C.C. Financing Statement (from Chapter 14)
- Security Agreement (from Chapter 14)
- Warranty Deed (from Chapter 11)
- Promissory Note (from Chapter 15)
- Bill of Sale (from Chapter 10)
- Assignment of Lease (from Chapter 8)
- Bulk Transfer Affidavit (from Chapter 17)
- Bulk Transfer Notice (from Chapter 17)

Agreement for Sale of Business Assets: This form should be used when one party is purchasing only certain business assets from another party. As in the previous form, this form, as it is shown in this book, is set up for use in the sale of sole proprietorship assets to an individual. This structure may be easily adapted to fit other particular situations if necessary. For example, if the business assets are being sold by a partnership and the buyer is a corporation, a few simple substitutions will be necessary to change the document to the appropriate form. Simply substitute the name and address of the partnership for the seller's name wherever indicated, substitute the name and address of the corporate buyer where necessary, and provide the proper signature lines as shown in Chapter 4. *Note*: Notarization is not provided for this form. Notarization of this form is only necessary if the sale of the business assets includes the sale of real estate. In that case, a notarization will be needed in order to record this document with the appropriate county real estate records office.

The following information will have to be used to fill in this form:

- Name and address of the seller
- Name and address of the buyer
- Type, name, and address of business of the seller
- A complete list of the business assets being sold

- The total amount being paid for the assets
- How this total amount is allocated among the assets being sold
- How the total amount will be paid
  - The amount of earnest money
  - The amount of downpayment paid at closing
  - The amount of a promissory note
    - The interest rate of the note
    - The term of the note
    - The amount of monthly payments of the note
- The closing date of the sale
- The location of the closing of the sale
- The documents of sale that the seller will provide at closing
- Any adjustments to the sale price that must be made at closing
- An accounting balance sheet of the business
- The terms of an agreement not to compete with the buyer
  - How long such an agreement will last
  - The geographical area covered by the agreement
- The amount of insurance the buyer agrees to carry on the business
- Any additional terms of agreement the parties wish to include
- The name of the state whose laws will govern the agreement

Note that you may also need to use the following additional documents in conjunction with the basic Agreement for Sale of Business Assets form:

- Exhibit A and/or B (Contract Exhibit form from Chapter 19)
- U.C.C. Financing Statement (from Chapter 14)
- Security Agreement (from Chapter 14)
- Promissory Note (from Chapter 15)
- Bill of Sale (from Chapter 10)
- Bulk Transfer Affidavit (from Chapter 17)
- Bulk Transfer Notice (from Chapter 17)

Agreement Not to Compete: This form, although not actually used to transfer ownership of any business assets, may often be used separately during the course of various business transfer transactions. It provides for the party who is selling a business or business assets to agree not to operate a similar business which will compete with the buyer. The terms include a geographical limitation (in terms of miles of radius) on how closely such a competing business can be operated. Also included is a time limit (in terms of years) that such an agreement will be in effect. The basic terms of this agreement not to compete are included in the previous two forms. This particular form should be used in those business situations in which an agreement not to compete is desired, but is not made in conjunction with the use of either of the above two documents.

Affidavit of Use of Fictitious Business Name: The registration of the use of a fictitious name is, in most jurisdictions, one of the only documents that needs to be completed prior to operating a business as a sole proprietorship. The purpose of this document is to place on a public record a statement verifying the actual name of the owner of a business that operates under a fictitious name. For example: if Ms. Jill Smith operates Golden Scissors Hair Styling Salon as a sole proprietorship, she would need to register her use of the fictitious name "Golden Scissors Hair Styling." This registration will allow any third party to check the public records and determine who is actually responsible for the business liabilities and debts. The rationale for this registration is to provide a public record of the name of the owner for the purpose of lawsuits.

The general method of registration follows two steps. First, a legal notice containing the information in the filed document must, generally, be run in a local newspaper for a specified number of times. This form (Notice of Intention to Use Fictitious Name) is provided on page 46. Second, the Affidavit, or registration form, is actually filed with the appropriate county records office. The legal affidavit provided for this registration should be valid in virtually all jurisdictions. However, certain locales may have slightly differing forms which must be used. Check with your local newspaper and with your county records office to see if the form provided is acceptable in your area.

To prepare this form, state the address of the business, the fictitious name of the business, and the name and percent of interest of all owners of the business. If there is more than one owner (for example, in a partnership) provide additional signature lines. This form should also have the appropriate notary acknowledgment form from Chapter 4.

Notice of Intention to Use Fictitious Name: As noted above, this form is merely a notice to be published in a local newspaper a certain number of times which publicly declares the intention of using a fictitious name in a business. This form is completed by filling in the address of the business, the fictitious name of the business, and the name and percent of interest of all owners of the business.

Partnership Agreement: This legal agreement is for use in beginning a partnership. This particular agreement provides for three partners to join into a partnership. Any number of partners, however, can be used with this agreement by simple addition or deletion of names and signature lines.

The information necessary to complete this form is as follows:

- The names and addresses of all partners
- The purpose of and description of the partnership
- The date on which the partnership will begin
- The name chosen for the partnership

- The amount and type (cash, services, or property) of capital that each partner will initially contribute to the partnership
- The date by which these contributions to the partnership must be made
- Whether the accounting for the partnership will be on an accrual or cash basis
- The proportionate shares of the profits and losses of the partnership that each partner will be entitled to
- Any additional terms of agreement that the parties wish to include
- The state whose laws will govern interpretation of the partnership agreement

Note that certain basic terms have been provided for the operation of the partnership under this agreement. These terms are general in nature and can be modified if all of the partners agree. The agreement terms which are provided are as follows:

- That additional contributions to capital may be made at any time by unanimous vote of the partners
- That each partner has equal management and control power
- That all decisions will be made by unanimous vote
- That the partners may select a partner to manage the day-to-day operations
- That bank checks may be signed by all of the partners or by the managing partner
- That the accounting will include income and capital accounts for each partner
- That partners can withdraw money from their income accounts only on unanimous agreement of the partners
- That a proportionate share of profits and losses is provided for
- That the partnership can be continued if a partner withdraws (or dies)
- That a withdrawing partner's interest must be sold to the remaining partners after an independent appraisal
- That a partner may not transfer any of his partnership interest to anyone else
- That the assets will be applied in a certain order to partnership obligations upon termination
- That mediation and arbitration will be used to settle disputes among the partners

Agreement for Sale of Business

This agreement is made on _____ , 20 _____ , between
_____ , seller, of
_____ ,
City of _____ , State of _____ , and
_____ , buyer, of
_____ ,
City of _____ , State of _____ .

The seller now owns and conducts a _____ business, under the name of
_____ , located at
_____ ,
City of _____ , State of _____ .

For valuable consideration, the seller agrees to sell and the buyer agrees to buy this business for the following price and on the following terms:

1. The seller will sell to the buyer, free from all liabilities, claims, and indebtedness, the seller's business, including the premises located at _____ ,
City of _____ , State of _____ , and all other assets of the business as listed on Exhibit A, which is attached and is a part of this agreement.

2. The buyer agrees to pay the seller the sum of $ _____ , which the seller agrees to accept as full payment. The purchase price will be allocated to the assets of the business as follows:

    a. The premises $ _____
    b. Equipment/furniture $ _____
    c. Goodwill $ _____
    d. Stock-in-trade/inventory $ _____
    e. Notes/accounts receivable $ _____
    f. Outstanding contracts $ _____

3. The purchase price will be paid as follows:

    Earnest money $ _____
    Cash downpayment $ _____
    Promissory note payable $ _____

    TOTAL Price $ _____

34

The $ _____ Promissory Note will bear interest at _____ %
(_____ percent) per year, payable monthly for _____ years at
$ _____ per month with the first payment due one (1) month after the
date of closing. The Promissory Note will be secured by a U.C.C. Financing Statement
and a Security Agreement in the usual commercial form. The Promissory Note will be
prepayable without limitation or penalty.

4. The seller acknowledges receiving the earnest money deposit of $ _____
   from the buyer. If this sale is not completed for any valid reason, this money will be returned
   to the buyer without penalty or interest.

5. This agreement will close on _____ , 20 _____ , at _____ o'clock
   _____ . m., at _____ ,
   City of _____ , State of _____ .

At that time, and upon payment by the buyer of the portion of the purchase price then due,
the seller will deliver to buyer the following documents:

   a. A Bill of Sale for all personal property (equipment, inventory, parts, supplies, and any
      other personal property)
   b. A Warranty Deed for any real estate
   c. All accounting books and records
   d. All customer and supplier lists
   e. A valid assignment of any lease
   f. All other documents of transfer as listed below:

At closing, adjustments to the purchase price will be made for the following items:

   a. Changes in inventory since this agreement was made
   b. Insurance premiums
   c. Payroll and payroll taxes
   d. Rental payments
   e. Utilities
   f. Property taxes
   g. The following other items:

6. The seller represents and warrants that it is duly qualified under the laws of the State of _____ to carry on the business being sold, and has complied with and is not in violation of any laws or regulations affecting the seller's business, including any laws governing bulk sales or transfers.

7. Attached as part of this agreement as Exhibit B is a Balance Sheet of the seller as of _____ , 20 _____ , which has been prepared according to generally accepted accounting principles. The seller warrants that this Balance Sheet fairly represents the financial position of the seller as of that date and sets out any contractual obligations of the seller. If this sale includes the sale of inventory of the business, the seller has provided the buyer with a completed Bulk Transfer Affidavit containing a complete list of all creditors of the seller, together with the amount claimed to be due to each creditor.

8. Seller represents that it has good and marketable title to all of the assets shown on Exhibit A, and that those assets are free and clear of any restrictions on transfer and all claims, taxes, indebtedness, or liabilities except those specified on the Exhibit B Balance Sheet. The seller also warrants that all equipment will be delivered in working order on the date of closing.

9. Seller agrees not to participate in any way, either directly or indirectly, in a business similar to that being sold to the buyer, within a radius of _____ miles from this business, for a period of _____ years from the date of closing.

10. Between the date of this agreement and the date of closing of the sale, the seller agrees to carry on the business in the usual manner and agrees not to enter into any unusual contract or other agreement affecting the operation of the business without the consent of the buyer.

11. The buyer represents that it is financially capable of completing the purchase of this business and fully understands its obligations under this agreement.

12. Buyer agrees to carry hazard and liability insurance on the assets of the business in the amount of $ _____ and to provide the seller with proof of this coverage until the Promissory Note is paid in full. However, the risk of any loss or damage to any assets being sold remain with the seller until the date of closing.

13. Any additional terms:

14. No modification of this agreement will be effective unless it is in writing and is signed by both the buyer and seller. This agreement binds and benefits both the buyer and seller and any successors. Time is of the essence of this agreement. This document, including any attachments, is the entire agreement between the buyer and seller. This agreement is governed by the laws of the State of _____ .

Dated: _____ , 20 _____

_____
Signature of Seller

_____
Printed Name of Seller

DBA

_____
Name of Business

A(n) _____ (type of business)

State of Operation _____

_____
Signature of Buyer

_____
Printed Name of Buyer

State of _____
County of _____

On _____ , 20 _____ , _____ personally came before me and, being duly sworn, did state that he or she is the person who owns the business described in the above document and that he or she signed the above document in my presence on behalf of the business and on his or her own behalf.

_____
Signature of Notary Public

Notary Public, In and for the County of _____
State of _____

My commission expires: _____ , 20 _____   Notary Seal

State of _____
County of _____

On _____ , 20 _____ , _____ personally
came before me and, being duly sworn, did state that he or she is the person described in the
above document as the buyer and that he or she signed the above document in my presence.

_____
Signature of Notary Public

Notary Public, In and for the County of _____
State of _____

My commission expires: _____ , 20 _____   Notary Seal

Agreement for Sale of Business Assets

This agreement is made on _____ , 20 _____ , between
_____ , seller, of
_____ ,
City of _____ , State of _____ , and
_____ , buyer, of
_____ ,
City of _____ , State of _____ .

The seller now owns and conducts a _____ business, under
the name of _____ , located at
_____ ,
City of _____ , State of _____ .

For valuable consideration, the seller agrees to sell and the buyer agrees to buy certain assets of this business for the following price and on the following terms:

1. The seller will sell to the buyer certain assets of the business as listed on Exhibit A, which is attached and is a part of this agreement. The assets will be transferred free from all liabilities, claims, and indebtedness, unless listed on Exhibit A.

2. The buyer agrees to pay the seller the sum of $ _____ , which the seller agrees to accept as full payment.

3. The purchase price will be paid as follows:

Earnest money	$	_____
Cash downpayment	$	_____
Promissory note payable	$	_____
TOTAL Price	$	_____

   The $ _____ Promissory Note will bear interest at _____ %
   (_____ percent) per year, payable monthly for _____ years at
   $ _____ per month with the first payment due one (1) month after the date of closing. The Promissory Note will be secured by a UCC Financing Statement and a Security Agreement in the usual commercial form. The Promissory Note will be prepayable without limitation or penalty.

4. The seller acknowledges receiving the earnest money deposit of $ _____ from the buyer. If this sale is not completed for any valid reason, this money will be returned to the buyer without penalty or interest.

5. This agreement will close on _____ , 20 _____ , at _____
   o'clock ___ . m., at _____ ,
   City of _____ , State of _____ .

   At that time, and upon payment by buyer of the portion of the purchase price then due, the seller will deliver to buyer the following documents:

   a. A Bill of Sale for all personal property (equipment, inventory, parts, supplies, and any other personal property)
   b. All other documents of transfer as listed below:

   At closing, adjustments to the purchase price will be made for changes in inventory since this agreement was made, and for the following other items:

6. The seller represents and warrants that it is in full compliance with and is not in violation of any laws or regulations affecting the seller's business, including any laws governing bulk sales or transfers.

7. Seller represents that it has good and marketable title to all of the assets shown on Exhibit A, and that those assets are free and clear of any restrictions on transfer, claims, taxes, indebtedness, or liabilities except those specified on the Exhibit A. If this sale includes the sale of inventory of the business, the seller has provided the buyer with a completed Bulk Transfer Affidavit containing a complete list of all creditors of the seller, together with the amount claimed to be due to each creditor. Seller also warrants that all equipment will be delivered in working order on the date of closing.

8. Between the date of this agreement and the date of closing of the sale, the seller agrees to carry on the business in the usual manner and agrees not to enter into any unusual contract or other agreement affecting the business assets being sold without the consent of the buyer.

9. The buyer represents that it is financially capable of completing the purchase of these business assets and fully understands its obligations under this agreement.

10. Buyer agrees to carry hazard and liability insurance on the assets of the business in the amount of $ _____ and to provide the seller with proof of this coverage until the Promissory Note is paid in full. However, the risk of any loss or damage to any assets being sold remain with the seller until the date of closing.

11. Any additional terms:

12. No modification of this agreement will be effective unless it is in writing and is signed by both the buyer and seller. This agreement binds and benefits both the buyer and seller and any successors. Time is of the essence of this agreement. This document, including any attachments, is the entire agreement between the buyer and seller. This agreement is governed by the laws of the State of _____ .

Dated: _____ , 20 _____

_____
Signature of Seller

_____
Printed Name of Seller

DBA
_____
Name of Business

A(n) _____ (type of business)

State of Operation _____

_____
Signature of Buyer

_____
Printed Name of Buyer

Agreement Not to Compete

This agreement is made on _____ , 20 _____ , between
_____ , seller, of
_____ ,
City of _____ , State of _____ , and
_____ , buyer, of
_____ ,
City of _____ , State of _____ .

The seller now owns and conducts a _____ business, under
the name of _____ , located at
_____ ,
City of _____ , State of _____ .

For valuable consideration, the buyer and seller agree as follows:

1. The seller agrees not to compete, either directly or indirectly, with the business of the buyer for a period of _____ years from the date of this agreement.

2. This agreement will only extend for a radius of _____ miles from the present location of the business of the buyer.

3. The seller agrees that "not to compete" means that the seller will not engage in any manner in a business or activity similar to that of the buyer's.

4. If the seller violates this agreement, the buyer will be entitled to an injunction to prevent such competition, without the need for the buyer to post any bond. In addition, the buyer will be entitled to any other legal relief.

5. Any additional terms:

42

6. No modification of this agreement will be effective unless it is in writing and is signed by both the buyer and seller. This agreement binds and benefits both the buyer and seller and any successors. Time is of the essence of this agreement. This document, including any attachments, is the entire agreement between the buyer and seller. This agreement is governed by the laws of the State of _____ .

Dated: _____ , 20 _____

_____
Signature of Seller

_____
Printed Name of Seller

DBA

_____
Name of Business

A(n) _____ (type of business)

State of Operation _____

_____
Signature of Buyer

_____
Printed Name of Buyer

Affidavit of Use of Fictitious Business Name

State of _____

County of _____

It is hereby stated, under oath, that pursuant to law:

1. The undersigned intends to engage in business at the following address:

    under the fictitious name of:

2. The full and true name of every person with an interest in this business and the ownership interest of each person is as follows:

Name	Percent of Interest
_____	_____
_____	_____
_____	_____
_____	_____

3. A Proof of Publication of a Notice of Intention to Use a Fictitious Name is filed with this affidavit.

Dated: _____ , 20 _____

Signature of Owner(s)	*Printed Name of Owner(s)*
_____	_____
_____	_____
_____	_____
_____	_____

State of _____
County of _____

On _____ , 20 _____ , _____ personally
came before me and, being duly sworn, did state that he, she, or they is or are the person(s)
who own(s) the business described in the above document and that he, she, or they signed
the above document in my presence.

_____
Signature of Notary Public

Notary Public, In and for the County of _____
State of _____

My commission expires: _____ , 20 _____   Notary Seal

Notice of Intention to Use Fictitious Business Name

NOTICE is hereby given that the undersigned intends to engage in business at the following address:

under the fictitious business name of:

The full and true name of every person with an interest in this business and the ownership interest of each person is as follows:

Name	*Percent of Interest*
_____	_____
_____	_____
_____	_____
_____	_____

Dated: _____ , 20 _____

Signature of Owner(s)	*Printed Name of Owner(s)*
_____	_____
_____	_____
_____	_____

Partnership Agreement

This agreement is made on _____ , 20 _____ , between
_____ , of
_____ ,
City of _____ , State of _____ , and
_____ , of
_____ ,
City of _____ , State of _____ .

The parties to this agreement agree to carry on a partnership for the following purpose:

and under the following terms and conditions:

1. The partnership will begin on _____ , 20 _____ , and will continue indefinitely until terminated.

2. The name of the partnership will be _____ .

3. The start-up capital of the partnership will be a total of $ _____ . Each partner of the partnership will contribute the following property, services, or cash to this total amount:

Name	Cash/Services/Property	Value
_____	_____	$ _____
_____	_____	$ _____
_____	_____	$ _____
_____	_____	$ _____
_____	_____	

These contributions must be made by _____ , 20 _____ . The partners may decide, by unanimous vote, to contribute additional capital to the partnership at any time.

4. Each partner will have an equal right to manage and control the partnership. Partnership decisions will be made by unanimous vote. The partners can select one of the partners to carry on the day-to-day operations of the partnership.

5. The partnership will maintain a bank account. Checks may be signed by either all of the partners together or by a partner selected to carry on the day-to-day operations of the partnership.

6. The partnership will maintain accounting records which will be open to any partner for inspection. These records will include separate income and capital accounts for each partner. The accounting will be on the _____ basis and on a calendar-year basis. The capital account of each partner will consist of no less than the value of the property, services, or cash contributed under paragraph 3 of this agreement. Partners may withdraw money from their income accounts upon unanimous agreement of the partners.

7. The profits and losses of the partnership will be shared by all partners in the following proportions:

Name	*Percent of Share*
_____	_____
_____	_____
_____	_____
_____	_____

8. If any partner withdraws from the partnership for any reason (including death), the partnership can continue and be operated by the remaining partners. However, the withdrawing partner (or his or her representative) will be obligated to sell his or her interest in the partnership to the remaining partners and the remaining partners will be obligated to buy that interest. The value of the withdrawing partner's interest will be his or her proportionate share of the total value of the partnership. The total value of the partnership will be determined by an independent appraisal made within ninety (90) days of the partner's withdrawal. All partners of the partnership (including the partner withdrawing) will equally share the cost of the appraisal.

9. A partner may not transfer all or part of his or her interest in the partnership to any other party.

10. The partnership may be terminated at any time by unanimous agreement among the partners. Upon termination, the partners agree to apply the assets and money of the partnership in the following order:

    a. to pay all the debts of the partnership
    b. to distribute the partner's income accounts to the partners in their proportionate share
    c. to distribute the partner's capital accounts to the partners in their proportionate share
    d. to distribute any remaining assets to the partners in their proportionate share

11. Any dispute between the partners related to this agreement will be settled by voluntary mediation. If mediation is unsuccessful, the dispute will be settled by binding arbitration using an arbitrator of the American Arbitration Association.

12. Any additional terms:

13. No modification of this agreement will be effective unless it is in writing and is signed by all partners. This agreement binds and benefits all partners and any successors. Time is of the essence of this agreement. This document is the entire agreement between the partners. This agreement is governed by the laws of the State of _____ .

Dated: _____ , 20 _____

Signature of Partner(s)   *Printed Name of Partner(s)*

_____ _____

_____ _____

_____ _____

_____ _____

CHAPTER 3
Contracts

The foundation of most business agreements is a contract. A *contract* is merely an agreement by which two or more parties each promise to do something. This simple definition of a contract can encompass incredibly complex agreements. The objective of a good business contract is to clearly set out the terms of the agreement. Once the parties have reached an oral understanding of what their agreement should be, the terms of the deal should be put in writing. Contrary to what many attorneys may tell you, the written contract should be clearly written and easily understood by both parties. It should be written in precise and unambiguous terms. The most common cause for litigation over contracts is arguments over the meaning of the language used. Remember that both sides to the agreement should be able to understand and agree to the language being used.

A contract has to have certain prerequisites to be enforceable in court. These requirements are relatively simple and most will be present in any standard agreement. However, you should understand what the various legal requirements are before you prepare your own contracts. To be enforceable, a contract must have *consideration*. In the context of contract law, this simply means that both parties to the contract must have promised to do something or forego taking some type of action. If one of the parties has not promised to do anything or forego any action, she or he will not be able to legally force the other party to comply with the terms of the contract. There has to be some form of mutual promise for a contract to be valid. For example: Party A agrees to pay Party B if Party B paints a car. Party A's promise is to pay if the job is completed. Party B's promise is to paint the car. If Party B paints the car and is not paid, Party A's promise to pay can be enforced in court. Similarly, if Party B fails to paint the car, Party A can have the contract enforced in court.

Another requirement is that the parties to the contract be clearly identified and the terms of the contract also be clearly spelled out. The terms and description need not be complicated, but they must be in enough detail to enable the parties to the contract (and any subsequent court) to clearly determine what exactly the parties were referring to when they made the contract. In the above example, the names and addresses of the parties must be included for the contract to be enforceable. In addition, a description of the car must be incorporated in the contract. Finally, a description of the type of paint job and the amount of money to be paid should also be contained in the contract.

Instructions

The following documents are included for use in situations requiring a basic contract. There are documents included for assigning, modifying, extending, and terminating a basic contract. A form for adding contract exhibits to contracts is included in Chapter 19.

Contract: This basic document can be adapted for use with many business situations. The terms of the contract to which the parties agree should be carefully spelled out and inserted where indicated. The other information required is the date the contract is to take effect and the names and addresses of the parties to the contract. This basic contract form is set up to accommodate an agreement between two individuals. It may, of course, be adapted for use between two business entities. Please use the appropriate signature lines from Chapter 4 if you wish to modify this basic form. If businesses are parties to the contract, please identify the name and type of business entity (for example: Jackson Car Stereo, a New York sole proprietorship, etc.) in the first section of the contract.

Extension of Contract: This document should be used to extend the effective time period during which a contract is in force. The use of this form allows the time limit to be extended without having to entirely re-draft the contract. Under this document, all of the other terms of the contract will remain the same, with only the expiration date changing. You will need to fill in the original expiration date and the new expiration date. Other information necessary will be the names and addresses of the parties to the contract and a description of the contract. A copy of the original contract should be attached to this form.

Modification of Contract: Use this form to modify any other terms of a contract (other than the expiration date). It can be used to change any portion of the contract. Simply note what changes are being made in the appropriate place on this form. If a portion of the contract is being deleted, make note of the deletion. If certain language is being substituted, state the substitution clearly. If additional language is being added, make this clear. A copy of the original contract should be attached to this form. For example, you may wish to use language as follows:

- "Paragraph _____ is deleted from this contract."
- "Paragraph _____ is deleted from this contract and the following paragraph is substituted in its place:"
- "The following new paragraph is added to this contract:"

Termination of Contract: This document is intended to be used when both parties to a contract mutually desire to end the contract prior to its original expiration date. Under this form, both parties agree to release each other from any claims against each other based on anything in the contract. This document effectively ends any contractual arrangement between two parties. Use the following information to complete this form: the names and addresses of the parties to the contract, a description of the contract, and the effective date of the termination of the contract.

Assignment of Contract: This form is for use if one party to a contract is assigning its full interest in the contract to another party. This effectively substitutes one party for another under a contract. This particular assignment form has both of the parties agreeing to indemnify and hold each other harmless for any failures to perform under the contract while they were the party liable under it. This *indemnify and hold harmless* clause simply means that if a claim arises for failure to perform, each party agrees to be responsible for the period of their own performance obligations. A description of the contract which is assigned should include the parties to the contract, the purpose of the contract, and the date of the contract. Use the following information to complete the assignment: the name and address of the *assignor* (the party who is assigning the contract), the name and address of the *assignee* (the party to whom the contract is being assigned), and the date of the assignment. A copy of the original contract should be attached to this form. A copy of a Consent to Assignment of Contract should also be attached, if necessary.

Consent to Assignment of Contract: This form is used if the original contract states that the consent of one of the parties is necessary for the assignment of the contract to be valid. A description of the contract and the name and signature of the person giving the consent are all that is necessary for completing this form. A copy of the original contract should be attached to this form.

Notice of Assignment of Contract: If a third party is involved in any of the contractual obligations or benefits of an assigned contract, that party should be notified of the assignment in writing. This alerts the third party to look to the new party for satisfaction of any obligations under the contract or to make any payments under the contract directly to the new party. Use the following information to complete this form: the names and addresses of the parties to the contract, a description of the contract, and the effective date of the assignment of the contract. A copy of the original contract should be attached to this form. A copy of a Consent to Assignment of Contract should also be attached, if necessary.

Notice of Breach of Contract: This form should be used to notify a party to a contract of the violation of a term of the contract or of an instance of failure to perform a required duty under the contract. It provides for a description of the alleged violation of the contract and for a time period in which the party is instructed to cure the breach of the contract. If the breach is not taken care of within the time period allowed, a lawyer should be consulted for further action, which may entail a lawsuit to enforce the contract terms. A copy of the original contract should be attached to this form.

Contract

This contract is made on _____ , 20 _____ ,
between _____ ,
address:

and _____ ,
address:

For valuable consideration, the parties agree as follows:

No modification of this contract will be effective unless it is in writing and is signed by both parties. This contract binds and benefits both parties and any successors. Time is of the essence of this contract. This document, including any attachments, is the entire agreement between the parties. This contract is governed by the laws of the State of _____ .

The parties have signed this contract on the date specified at the beginning of this contract.

_____   _____
Signature   Signature

_____   _____
Printed Name   Printed Name

Extension of Contract

This extension of contract is made on _____ , 20 _____ ,
between _____ ,
address:

and _____ ,
address:

For valuable consideration, the parties agree as follows:

1. The following described contract will end on _____ , 20 _____ :

    This contract is attached to this extension and is a part of this extension.

2. The parties agree to extend this contract for an additional period, which will begin
    immediately on the expiration of the original time period and will end on
    _____ , 20 _____ .

3. The extension of this contract will be on the same terms and conditions as the original
    contract. This extension binds and benefits both parties and any successors. This document,
    including the attached original contract, is the entire agreement between the parties.

The parties have signed this extension on the date specified at the beginning of this extension
of contract.

_____   _____
Signature   Signature

_____   _____
Printed Name   Printed Name

Modification of Contract

This modification of contract is made on _____ , 20 _____ ,
between _____ ,
address:

and _____ ,
address:

For valuable consideration, the parties agree as follows:

1. The following described contract is attached to this modification and is made a part of
   this modification:

2. The parties agree to modify this contract as follows:

3. All other terms and conditions of the original contract remain in effect without modification. This modification binds and benefits both parties and any successors. This document,
   including the attached contract, is the entire agreement between the parties.

The parties have signed this modification on the date specified at the beginning of this modification of contract.

_____   _____
Signature   Signature

_____   _____
Printed Name   Printed Name

Termination of Contract

This termination of contract is made on _____ , 20 _____ ,
between _____ ,
address:

and _____ ,
address:

For valuable consideration, the parties agree as follows:

1. The parties are currently bound under the terms of the following described contract, which is attached and is part of this termination:

2. They agree to mutually terminate and cancel this contract effective on this date. This termination agreement will act as a mutual release of all obligations under this contract for both parties, as if the contract has not been entered into in the first place.

3. This termination binds and benefits both parties and any successors. This document, including the attached contract being terminated, is the entire agreement between the parties.

The parties have signed this termination on the date specified at the beginning of this termination of contract.

_____   _____
Signature   Signature

_____   _____
Printed Name   Printed Name

Assignment of Contract

This assignment of contract is made on _____ , 20 _____ ,
between _____ ,
address:

and _____ ,
address:

For valuable consideration, the parties agree to the following terms and conditions:

1. The assignor assigns all interest, burdens, and benefits in the following described contract to the assignee:

    This contract is attached to this assignment and is a part of this assignment.

2. The assignor warrants that this contract is in effect, has not been modified, and is fully assignable. If the consent of a third party is necessary for this assignment to be effective, such consent is attached to this assignment and is a part of this assignment. Assignor agrees to indemnify and hold the assignee harmless from any claim which may result from the assignor's failure to perform under this contract prior to the date of this assignment.

3. The assignee agrees to perform all obligations of the assignor and receive all of the benefits of the assignor under this contract. Assignee agrees to indemnify and hold the assignor harmless from any claim which may result from the assignee's failure to perform under this contract after the date of this assignment.

4. This assignment binds and benefits both parties and any successors. This document, including any attachments, is the entire agreement between the parties.

The parties have signed this assignment on the date specified at the beginning of this assignment of contract.

_____   _____
Signature of Assignor   Signature of Assignee

_____   _____
Printed Name of Assignor   Printed Name of Assignee

Consent to Assignment of Contract

Date: _____ , 20 _____

To: _____

I am a party to the following described contract:

This contract is the subject of the attached assignment of contract.

I consent to the assignment of this contract as described in the attached assignment, which provides that the assignee is substituted for the assignor.

_____
Signature

_____
Printed Name

Notice of Assignment of Contract

Date: _____ , 20 _____

To: _____

RE: Assignment of Contract

Dear _____

This notice is in reference to the following described contract:

Please be advised that as of _____ , 20 _____ , all interest and rights under this contract which were formerly owned by
_____ , of
_____ ,
City of _____ , State of _____ , have been permanently
assigned to _____ , of
_____ ,
City of _____ , State of _____ .

Please be advised that all of the obligations and rights of the former party to this contract are now the responsibility of the new party to this contract.

_____
Signature

_____
Printed Name

Notice of Breach of Contract

Date: _____ , 20 _____

To: _____

RE: Breach of Contract

Dear _____

This notice is in reference to the following described contract:

Please be advised that as of _____ , 20 _____ , we are holding you in BREACH OF CONTRACT for the following reasons:

If this breach of contract is not corrected within _____ days of this notice, we will take further action to protect our rights, which may include the right to obtain a substitute service and charge you for any additional costs. This notice is made under the Uniform Commercial Code and any other applicable laws. All of our rights are reserved under this notice.

_____
Signature

_____
Printed Name

60

CHAPTER 4
Signatures and Notary Acknowledgments

Signatures and notary acknowledgments for legal forms serve similar but slightly different purposes. Both are used to document the formal signing of a legal instrument, but the notarized acknowledgment also serves as a method of providing a neutral witness to the signature, and so, authenticates the signature. In addition, a notarized acknowledgment can serve an additional purpose of providing a statement under oath. For example, a notarized acknowledgment can be used to assert that a person states, under oath, that he has read the document that she or he is signing and believes that what it contains is the truth.

The use of a notary acknowledgment is not required for all legal forms. The notary acknowledgments contained in this chapter are to be used only for the purpose of providing a notarization required for recording a document. Generally, notarization is only necessary if the document is intended to be recorded with an official government office in some manner. For example, all documents which intend to convey real estate should be recorded in the county recorder's office or register of deeds office in the county (or parish) where the property is located. In virtually all jurisdictions, such documents must be notarized before they will be recorded. Similarly, some states require automobile titles and similar documents to be notarized. Check with your local county clerk to determine the requirements in your locale.

Another unofficial purpose of notarization of legal documents is to make the document seem more important to the parties. By formally having their signatures witnessed by a notary public, they are attesting to the fact that they ascribe a powerful purpose to the document. Although this type of notarization carries with it no legal value, it does serve a valid purpose in solemnizing the signing of an important business document.

For all of the notary acknowledgment forms contained in this chapter, the following information is necessary:

- The name of the state in which the document is signed
- The name of the county in which the document is signed
- The date on which the document is signed
- The name of the person who is signing the document
- The entity on whose behalf the person is signing (for example: a corporation, partnership, etc.)
- The name of the notary public (or similar official)

- The county in which the notary is registered to act
- The state in which the notary is authorized to perform
- The date on which the notary's commission will expire

In addition, many states require that the notary place an embossed seal on the document to authenticate the notarization process. The notary who completes the acknowledgment will know the correct procedure for your state.

A simple signature line merely serves to provide a place for a party to a document to sign his or her name. However, care must be taken to be sure that the type of signature line used corresponds exactly with the person or business entity who is joining in the signing of a document. If the entity is a partnership, the signature must be set up for a partner to sign and clearly state that the signature is for the partnership. The same holds true for the signature of a corporate officer.

Instructions

The following notary acknowledgments and signature lines are intended to be used for the specific purposes outlined below. When preparing a legal document, choose the correct version of these additions carefully. The following are contained in this chapter:

Corporate Acknowledgment: This clause should be used on documents where a corporation is one of the parties who is to sign the document and the document needs to be notarized. The person signing the document on behalf of the corporation must be either an officer of the corporation or be specifically authorized by a resolution of the Board of Directors of the corporation to act on its behalf.

Corporate Signature Line: This line should be inserted on all documents where a party that will sign the document is a corporation. This may be used regardless of whether the corporation is a corporation, an S-corporation, or a not-for-profit corporation. The person signing must have authority to bind the corporation. Again, it must either be an officer of the corporation or a person specifically authorized by a resolution of the Board of Directors of the corporation to act on its behalf. The state in which the corporation is registered to do business should be noted.

Partnership Acknowledgment: This clause should be used on documents where one of the parties who is to sign the document is a standard partnership and the document needs to be notarized. Any partner in a partnership may have authority to act on behalf of the corporation. However, it may be wise to request a copy of the partnership agreement which authorizes the partner to bind the partnership.

Partnership Signature Line: This line should be inserted on all documents where one of the parties that will sign the document is a partnership. This may be used if the entity is a partnership. Any partner may bind the partnership if authorized by the partnership agreement. The state in which the partnership is doing business should be noted.

Limited Liability Company Acknowledgment: This clause should be used on documents where a limited liability company is one of the parties who is to sign the document and the document needs to be notarized. Any member of a limited liability company has authority to bind the limited partnership.

Limited Liability Company Signature Line: This line should be inserted on all documents where one of the parties who will sign the document is a limited liability company. Any member may sign on behalf of a limited liability company. The state in which the limited liability company is doing business should be noted.

Sole Proprietorship Acknowledgment: This clause should be used on documents where an individual who owns a sole proprietorship is one of the parties who is to sign the document and the document needs to be notarized. Many sole proprietorships are designated as persons "doing business as." This is abbreviated as "DBA." For example: "John Washington, DBA Washington's Restaurant" indicates that John Washington is operating Washington's Restaurant as a sole proprietorship. The owner of the sole proprietorship is the person who should sign all documents for this type of business.

Sole Proprietorship Signature Line: This line should be inserted on all documents where a party that will sign the document is an individual that owns a sole proprietorship. Only the owner of a sole proprietorship has authority to bind such a business. The state in which the sole proprietorship is doing business should be noted.

Power of Attorney Acknowledgment: This clause should be used on documents where an individual acting under a power of attorney is one of the parties who is to sign the document and the document needs to be notarized. As noted in Chapter 5, an *attorney-in-fact* is a person who is authorized to act for another person by virtue of a document entitled a "Power of Attorney," also found in Chapter 5.

Power of Attorney Signature Line: This line should be inserted on all documents where a party that will sign the document is an individual acting under a power of attorney. The person signing must have the specific authority to act for another person under some form of Power of Attorney. The date of the Power of Attorney form should be noted.

Individual Acknowledgment: This clause should be used on documents where an individual is one of the parties who is to sign the document and the document needs to be notarized. However, if the document is to be signed by a husband and wife together, use the appropriate acknowledgment form which follows.

Individual Signature Line: This line should be inserted on all documents where a party that will sign the document is an individual. Again, however, if the document is to be signed by a husband and wife together, use the appropriate signature line which follows.

Husband and Wife Acknowledgment: This clause should be used on documents where both a husband and wife are to sign the document and the document needs to be notarized.

Husband and Wife Signature Line: This line should be inserted on all documents where both a husband and wife are intended to sign the document.

Corporate Acknowledgment

State of _____

County of _____

On _____ , 20 _____ , _____
personally came before me and, being duly sworn, did state that he or she is the
_____ of the corporation described in the above document;
that he or she signed the above document in my presence on behalf of this corporation; and that he or she had full authority to do so.

_____
Signature of Notary Public

Notary Public, In and for the County of _____
State of _____

My commission expires: _____   Notary Seal

Corporate Signature Line

_____ (*name of corporation*), a(n)
_____ (*state of incorporation*) corporation

By:

_____
Signature of Corporate Officer

_____
Printed Name of Corporate Officer

The _____ (*title of corporate officer*) of the corporation

Partnership Acknowledgment

State of _____

County of _____

On _____, 20 _____, _____
personally came before me and, being duly sworn, did state that he or she is a
partner of the partnership described in the above document; that he or she signed
the above document in my presence on behalf of this partnership; and that he or
she had full authority to do so.

_____
Signature of Notary Public

Notary Public, In and for the County of _____
State of _____

My commission expires: _____   Notary Seal

Partnership Signature Line

_____ (*name of partnership*), a(n)
_____ (*state of operation*) partnership

By:

_____
Signature of Partner

_____
Printed Name of Partner

A Partner of the Partnership

Limited Liability Company Acknowledgment

State of _____
County of _____

On _____ , 20 _____ , _____
personally came before me and, being duly sworn, did state that he or she is a member of the limited liability company described in the above document; that he or she signed the above document in my presence on behalf of this limited liability company; and that he or she had full authority to do so.

_____
Signature of Notary Public

Notary Public, In and for the County of _____
State of _____

My commission expires: _____   Notary Seal

Limited Liability Company Signature Line

_____ (*name of limited liability company*), a(n)
_____ (*state of operation*) limited liability company

By:

_____
Signature of Member

_____
Printed Name of Member

A Member of the Limited Liability Company

Sole Proprietorship Acknowledgment

State of _____

County of _____

On _____ , 20 _____ , _____
personally came before me and, being duly sworn, did state that he or she is the
person who owns the sole proprietorship described in the above document and
that he or she signed the above document in my presence on behalf of the sole
proprietorship and on his or her own behalf.

_____
Signature of Notary Public

Notary Public, In and for the County of _____
State of _____

My commission expires: _____   Notary Seal

Sole Proprietorship Signature Line

_____
Signature of Sole Proprietor

_____
Printed Name of Sole Proprietor

DBA _____ (*name of business*), a(n)
_____ (*state of operation*) sole proprietorship

Power of Attorney Acknowledgment

State of _____

County of _____

On _____ , 20 _____ , _____
personally came before me and, being duly sworn, did state that he or she is the
attorney-in-fact of _____ described in the above
document; that he or she signed the above document in my presence as attorney-
in-fact on behalf of this person; and that he or she had full authority to do so under
Power of Attorney dated _____ , 20 _____ .

_____
Signature of Notary Public

Notary Public, In and for the County of _____
State of _____

My commission expires: _____   Notary Seal

Power of Attorney Signature Line

_____
Signature of Person Holding Power of Attorney

_____
Printed Name of Person Holding Power of Attorney

As attorney-in-fact for _____ (*name of person
granting power of attorney*)

Under Power of Attorney dated _____ , 20 _____

Individual Acknowledgment

State of _____

County of _____

On _____ , 20 _____ , _____
personally came before me and, being duly sworn, did state that he or she is the
person described in the above document and that he or she signed the above document in my presence as a free and voluntary act for the purposes stated.

_____
Signature of Notary Public

Notary Public, In and for the County of _____
State of _____

My commission expires: _____   Notary Seal

Individual Signature Line

_____
Signature

_____
Printed Name

Husband and Wife Acknowledgment

State of _____
County of _____

On _____ , 20 _____ , _____
and _____ personally came before me and, being
duly sworn, did state that they are the husband and wife described in the above
document and that they signed the above document in my presence as a free and
voluntary act for the purposes stated.

_____
Signature of Notary Public

Notary Public, In and for the County of _____
State of _____

My commission expires: _____   Notary Seal

Husband and Wife Signature Line

_____   _____
Signature of Husband   Signature of Wife

_____   _____
Printed Name of Husband   Printed Name of Wife

CHAPTER 5
Powers of Attorney

A *power of attorney* form is a document that is used to allow one person to give the authority to act on his or her behalf to another person. The person signing the power of attorney grants legal authority to another person to "stand in his or her shoes" and act legally for him or her. The person who receives the power of attorney is called an *attorney-in-fact*. However, this title and the power of attorney form does not mean that the person receiving the power has to be a lawyer.

Power of attorney forms are useful documents for many occasions. They can be used to authorize someone else to sign certain documents if you cannot be present when the signatures are necessary. For example, a real estate closing in another state can be completed without your presence by providing a power of attorney to a real estate agent (or even a friend) that authorizes him or her to sign the documents on your behalf. Similarly, if you must be away from your home on a trip, and certain actions must be made in your absence, a power of attorney can be granted to enable another person to legally perform on your behalf. The form can also be used to allow your accountant to negotiate with the Internal Revenue Service, allow your secretary to sign checks and temporarily operate your business, or for many other purposes.

Traditionally, property matters were the type of actions handled with powers of attorney. Increasingly, however, people are using a specific type of power of attorney to authorize other persons to act on their behalf in the event of disability. This broad type of power of attorney is called a *durable power of attorney*. A durable power of attorney is intended to remain in effect even if a person becomes disabled or incompetent. All states have passed legislation that specifically authorizes this type of power of attorney. The durable power of attorney forms that are included in this book are intended to be used to allow another person to handle financial matters for an incapacitated person. The forms and the powers that these forms provide only go into effect upon the certification by one's primary physician that the person granting the power is incapacitated. Both the unlimited and limited durable power of attorney forms require notarization of the forms and the use of two witnesses to the signature, even though this in not a technical requirement in all states. The use of a notary public and witnesses will generally prevent delays or challenges to the powers that are granted in the durable power of attorney. Please note that these durable power of attorney forms are not intended to be used to make healthcare decisions on behalf of another person. The legal form that allows another person to make various healthcare decisions on behalf of an incapacitated person is referred to as a *durable power of attorney for healthcare*. This type of form is beyond the scope of this book and is not included. Please refer to Nova Publishing Company's *Living Wills Simplified*, by Dan Sitarz, for information on preparing this type of form. *Note*: Powers of attorney are very powerful legal documents. They can be used to grant virtually unlimited legal power to another person. You are advised to proceed with caution when using any of these forms. If you have any questions regarding their use, please consult a competent attorney.

Instructions

Unlimited Power of Attorney: This form should be used only in situations where you desire to authorize another person to act for you in *all* transactions. The grant of power under this document is unlimited. However, please be advised that some states may require that you specifically spell out the authority granted to perform certain acts. Generally, however, for personal and property transactions, this broad grant of power will be effective. All that is necessary are the names and addresses of both the person granting the power and the person receiving the power. Both persons should sign the document. The signature of the person granting the power should be notarized and witnessed by two people.

Limited Power of Attorney: This document provides for a *limited* grant of authority to another person. It should be used in those situations when you need to authorize another person to act for you in a specific manner or to perform a specific action. The type of acts that you authorize the other person to perform should be spelled out in detail to avoid confusion (for example, to sign any necessary forms to complete the closing of the sale of real estate). What is needed to complete this form are the names and addresses of the person granting the power and the person receiving the power, and a full and detailed description of the powers granted. Both persons should sign the document. The signature of the person granting the power should be notarized and witnessed by two people.

Durable Unlimited Power of Attorney: Like the Unlimited Power of Attorney described above, this form should be used only in a situation in which you desire to authorize another person to act for you in *all* transactions. The grant of power under this document is unlimited. However, unlike the general Unlimited Power of Attorney, this form remains in effect *even* if you are incapacitated or disabled. This broad grant of power will be effective to allow your attorney-in-fact to perform on your behalf in the event of your disability. To complete this form, the name and address of the person granting the power and also of the person receiving the power should be filled in. Both persons should sign the document. The signature of the person granting the power should be notarized and witnessed by two other persons at the same time. The person receiving the power of attorney cannot be one of the witnesses.

Durable Limited Power of Attorney: Like the Limited Power of Attorney described previously, this document provides for a *limited* grant of authority to another person. It should be used in those situations where you need to authorize another to act for you in a specific manner or to perform a specific action. However, this form remains in effect *even* if you are incapacitated or disabled. The limited grant of power provided by this document will be effective to allow your attorney-in-fact to perform on your behalf in the event of your disability. To complete this form, the names and addresses of both the person granting the power and the person receiving the power should be filled in. A full and detailed description of the powers granted should be inserted. Both persons should sign the document. The signature of the person granting the power should be notarized and witnessed by two other persons at the same time. The person receiving the power of attorney cannot be one of the witnesses.

Revocation of Power of Attorney: This document may be used with any of the previous four power of attorney forms. The revocation is used to terminate the original authority that was granted to the other person in the first place. If the grant of power was for a limited purpose and that purpose is complete, this revocation should be used as soon after the transaction as possible. In any event, if you choose to revoke a power of attorney, a copy of this revocation should be provided to the person to whom the power was given. Copies should also be given to any party that may have had dealings with the attorney-in-fact before the revocation and to any party with whom the attorney-in-fact may be expected to attempt to deal with after the revocation.

Unlimited Power of Attorney

I, _____ ,
address:

grant an unlimited power of attorney to _____ ,
address:

to act as my attorney-in-fact.

I give my attorney-in-fact the maximum power under law to perform any act on my behalf that I could do personally, including but not limited to, all acts relating to any and all of my financial transactions and/or business affairs including all banking and financial institution transactions, all real estate or personal property transactions, all insurance or annuity transactions, all claims and litigation, and any and all business transactions. My attorney-in-fact is granted full power to act on my behalf in the same manner as if I were personally present. My attorney-in-fact accepts this appointment and agrees to act in my best interest as he or she considers advisable. This power of attorney may be revoked by me at any time and is automatically revoked upon my death or incapacitation. My attorney-in-fact shall not be compensated for his or her services nor shall my attorney-in-fact be liable to me, my estate, heirs, successors, or assigns for acting or refraining from acting under this document, except for willful misconduct or gross negligence. Any third party who receives a signed copy of this document may act under it. Revocation of this document is not effective unless a third party has actual knowledge of such revocation.

Dated _____ , 20 _____

_____
Signature of Person Granting Power of Attorney

_____
Printed Name of Person Granting Power of Attorney

_____   _____
Signature of Witness #1   Signature of Witness #2

_____   _____
Printed Name of Witness #1   Printed Name of Witness #2

State of _____
County of _____

On _____ , 20 _____ , _____ personally
came before me and, being duly sworn, did state that he or she is the person described in the
above document and that he or she signed the above document in my presence.

_____
Signature of Notary Public

Notary Public, In and for the County of _____
State of _____

My commission expires: _____   Notary Seal

I accept my appointment as attorney-in-fact.

_____
Signature of Person Granted Power of Attorney

_____
Printed Name of Person Granted Power of Attorney

Limited Power of Attorney

I, _____ ,
address:

grant a limited power of attorney to _____ ,
address:

to act as my attorney-in-fact.

I give my attorney-in-fact the maximum power under law to perform the following specific acts on my behalf:

My attorney-in-fact accepts this appointment and agrees to act in my best interest as he or she considers advisable. This power of attorney may be revoked by me at any time and is automatically revoked upon my death or incapacitation. My attorney-in-fact shall not be compensated for his or her services nor shall my attorney-in-fact be liable to me, my estate, heirs, successors, or assigns for acting or refraining from acting under this document, except for willful misconduct or gross negligence. Any third party who receives a signed copy of this document may act under it. Revocation of this document is not effective unless a third party has actual knowledge of such revocation.

Dated _____ , 20 _____

_____
Signature of Person Granting Power of Attorney

_____
Printed Name of Person Granting Power of Attorney

_____   _____
Signature of Witness #1   Signature of Witness #2

_____   _____
Printed Name of Witness #1   Printed Name of Witness #2

State of _____
County of _____

On _____ , 20 _____ , _____ personally
came before me and, being duly sworn, did state that he or she is the person described in the
above document and that he or she signed the above document in my presence.

_____
Signature of Notary Public

Notary Public, In and for the County of _____
State of _____

My commission expires: _____   Notary Seal

I accept my appointment as attorney-in-fact.

_____
Signature of Person Granted Power of Attorney

_____
Printed Name of Person Granted Power of Attorney

Durable Unlimited Power of Attorney

I, _____ ,
address:

grant an unlimited durable power of attorney to _____ ,
address:

to act as my attorney-in-fact.

This power of attorney shall become effective upon my incapacitation, as certified by my primary physician, or if my primary physician is not available, by any other attending physician. This power of attorney grants no power or authority regarding healthcare decisions to my designated attorney-in-fact. I give my attorney-in-fact the maximum power under law to perform any act on my behalf that I could do personally, including but not limited to, all acts relating to any and all of my financial transactions and/or business affairs including all banking and financial institution transactions, all real estate or personal property transactions, all insurance or annuity transactions, all claims and litigation, and any and all business transactions. My attorney-in-fact is granted full power to act on my behalf in the same manner as if I were personally present. My attorney-in-fact accepts this appointment and agrees to act in my best interest as he or she considers advisable. This power of attorney may be revoked by me at any time and is automatically revoked upon my death. This power of attorney shall not be affected by my present or future disability or incapacity. My attorney-in-fact shall not be compensated for his or her services nor shall my attorney-in-fact be liable to me, my estate, heirs, successors, or assigns for acting or refraining from acting under this document, except for willful misconduct or gross negligence. Any third party who receives a signed copy of this document may act under it. Revocation of this document is not effective unless a third party has actual knowledge of such revocation.

Dated _____ , 20 _____

_____
Signature of Person Granting Power of Attorney

_____
Printed Name of Person Granting Power of Attorney

_____   _____
Signature of Witness #1   Signature of Witness #2

_____   _____
Printed Name of Witness #1   Printed Name of Witness #2

State of _____
County of _____

On _____ , 20 _____ , _____ personally
came before me and, being duly sworn, did state that he or she is the person described in the
above document and that he or she signed the above document in my presence.

_____
Signature of Notary Public

Notary Public, In and for the County of _____
State of _____

My commission expires: _____   Notary Seal

I accept my appointment as attorney-in-fact.

_____
Signature of Person Granted Power of Attorney

_____
Printed Name of Person Granted Power of Attorney

80

Durable Limited Power of Attorney

I, _____ ,
address:

grant a limited durable power of attorney to _____ ,
address:

to act as my attorney-in-fact.

I give my attorney-in-fact the maximum power under law to perform the following specific acts on my behalf:

This power of attorney shall become effective upon my incapacitation, as certified by my primary physician, or if my primary physician is not available, by any other attending physician. This power of attorney grants no power or authority regarding healthcare decisions to my designated attorney-in-fact. My attorney-in-fact accepts this appointment and agrees to act in my best interest as he or she considers advisable. This power of attorney may be revoked by me at any time and is automatically revoked upon my death. This power of attorney shall not be affected by my present or future disability or incapacity. My attorney-in-fact shall not be compensated for his or her services nor shall my attorney-in-fact be liable to me, my estate, heirs, successors, or assigns for acting or refraining from acting under this document, except for willful misconduct or gross negligence. Any third party who receives a signed copy of this document may act under it. Revocation of this document is not effective unless a third party has actual knowledge of such revocation.

Dated _____ , 20 _____

_____
Signature of Person Granting Power of Attorney

_____
Printed Name of Person Granting Power of Attorney

_____   _____
Signature of Witness #1   Signature of Witness #2

_____   _____
Printed Name of Witness #1   Printed Name of Witness #2

State of _____

County of _____

On _____ , 20 _____ , _____ personally came before me and, being duly sworn, did state that he or she is the person described in the above document and that he or she signed the above document in my presence.

_____
Signature of Notary Public

Notary Public, In and for the County of _____
State of _____

My commission expires: _____   Notary Seal

I accept my appointment as attorney-in-fact.

_____
Signature of Person Granted Power of Attorney

_____
Printed Name of Person Granted Power of Attorney

Revocation of Power of Attorney

I, _____ ,
address:

revoke the power of attorney dated _____ , 20 _____ ,
which was granted to _____ ,
address:

to act as my attorney-in-fact.

Dated _____ , 20 _____

_____
Signature of Person Revoking Power of Attorney

_____
Printed Name of Person Revoking Power of Attorney

State of _____
County of _____

On _____ , 20 _____ , _____ personally
came before me and, being duly sworn, did state that he or she is the person described in the
above document and that he or she signed the above document in my presence.

_____
Signature of Notary Public

Notary Public, In and for the County of _____
State of _____

My commission expires: _____   Notary Seal

CHAPTER 6
Releases

Releases are a method of acknowledging the satisfaction of an obligation or of releasing parties from liability or claims. Releases are used in various situations in the business world, from releasing a person or company from liability after an accident to a release of liens or claims against property. They can be a useful means of settling minor disputes. One party may pay another to release a claim. For example: Party A pays Party B $200.00 to release its claims for damages incurred when Party A's truck damaged Party B's garage.

Releases can be very powerful documents. The various releases contained in this chapter are tailored to meet the most common situations in which a release is used. For a release to be valid, there must be some type of consideration received by the person who is granting the release. Releases should be used carefully as they may prevent any future claims against the party to whom it is granted. In general, a release from claims relating to an accident which causes personal injury should not be signed without a prior examination by a doctor. Also note that a release relating to damage to community property in a "community property" state must be signed by both spouses. Study the various forms provided to determine which one is proper for the use intended. Please note that other chapters in this book also contain specific release forms which are intended to be used in specific business financing situations. Chapter 14 contains two additional releases: Release of Security Interest and Release of U.C.C. Financing Statement; Chapter 15 contains a Release of Promissory Note; and Chapter 20 contains a Model's Photographic Release. Please refer to those chapters for an explanation of these particular release forms.

Instructions

The following releases are included in this chapter:

General Release: This release serves as a full blanket-release from one party to another. It should only be used when all obligations of one party are to be released. The party signing this release is discharging the other party from all of their obligations to the other party stemming from a specific incident or transaction. This form can be used when one party has a claim against another and the other agrees to waive the claim for payment.

Mutual Release: The mutual release form provides a method for two parties to jointly release each other from their mutual obligations or claims. This form should be used when both parties intend to discharge each other from all of their mutual obligations. It essentially serves the purpose of two reciprocal General Releases.

Specific Release: This release form should be used only when a particular claim or obligation is being released, while allowing other liabilities to continue. The obligation being released should be spelled out in careful and precise terms to prevent confusion with any other obligation or claim. In addition, the liabilities which are not being released, but will survive, should also be carefully noted.

Release of Mechanic's Liens: This type of release will be used in the specific situation of verifying that there are no outstanding contractor's or mechanic's claims against a property for any goods or services provided in conjunction with work on the property. If there have been subcontractors or suppliers involved in connection with the work provided, all such parties should sign this release. This release does not relieve the party to whom it is given from paying for any goods and services which have been provided. It merely releases the property itself from any potential liens by the contractors or suppliers. A complete and definite description of the property to which the release applies must be included. Since this document may be recorded, it should generally be notarized. The form provided contains a general individual acknowledgment and signature form for each of the contractors signing. However, if the person signing the release is signing other than as an individual (for example: a partner signing for a partnership), the appropriate acknowledgment and signature form from Chapter 4 must be used instead.

General Release

For consideration, I, _____ ,
address:

release _____ ,
address:

from all claims and obligations, known or unknown, to this date arising from the following
transaction or incident:

The party signing this release has not assigned any claims or obligations covered by this
release to any other party.

The party signing this release intends that it both bind and benefit itself and any successors.

Dated _____ , 20 _____

_____
Signature

_____
Printed Name

Mutual Release

For consideration, _____ ,
address:

and _____ ,
address:

release each other from all claims and obligations, known or unknown, that they may have against each other arising from the following transaction or incident:

Neither party has assigned any claims or obligations covered by this release to any other party.

Both parties signing this release intend that it both bind and benefit themselves and any successors.

Dated _____ , 20 _____

_____   _____
Signature   Signature

_____   _____
Printed Name   Printed Name

Specific Release

For consideration, I, _____ ,
address:

release _____ ,
address:

from the following specific claims and obligations:

arising from the following transaction or incident:

Any claims or obligations that are not specifically mentioned are not released by this Specific Release.

The party signing this release has not assigned any claims or obligations covered by this release to any other party.

The party signing this release intends that it both bind and benefit itself and any successors.

Dated _____ , 20 _____

_____
Signature

_____
Printed Name

Release of Mechanic's Liens

The following contractors or subcontractors have furnished materials, labor, or both for construction at the property owned by_____ ,
of _____ ,
City of _____ , State of _____ :

Contractor/Subcontractor	Address	City	State/Zip
_____	_____	_____	_____
_____	_____	_____	_____
_____	_____	_____	_____
_____	_____	_____	_____
_____	_____	_____	_____

These contractors or subcontractors hereby release all liens and the right to file any liens against this property for material or labor provided as of this date. This release does not, however, constitute a release of any sums which may be due to these contractors or subcontractors for materials or labor.

The parties signing this release intend that it both bind and benefit themselves and any successors.

Dated: _____ , 20 _____

_____   _____
Signature   Printed Name

_____   _____
Signature   Printed Name

_____   _____
Signature   Printed Name

_____   _____
Signature   Printed Name

_____   _____
Signature   Printed Name

State of _____
County of _____

On _____ , 20 _____ , _____ personally came before me and, being duly sworn, did state that he or she is the person described in the above document and that he or she signed the above document in my presence.

_____
Signature of Notary Public

Notary Public, In and for the County of _____
State of _____

My commission expires: _____ , 20 _____   Notary Seal

State of _____
County of _____

On _____ , 20 _____ , _____ personally came before me and, being duly sworn, did state that he or she is the person described in the above document and that he or she signed the above document in my presence.

_____
Signature of Notary Public

Notary Public, In and for the County of _____
State of _____

My commission expires: _____ , 20 _____   Notary Seal

State of _____
County of _____

On _____ , 20 _____ , _____ personally came before me and, being duly sworn, did state that he or she is the person described in the above document and that he or she signed the above document in my presence.

_____
Signature of Notary Public

Notary Public, In and for the County of _____
State of _____

My commission expires: _____ , 20 _____   Notary Seal

State of _____
County of _____

On _____ , 20 _____ , _____ personally
came before me and, being duly sworn, did state that he or she is the person described in the
above document and that he or she signed the above document in my presence.

_____
Signature of Notary Public

Notary Public, In and for the County of _____
State of _____

My commission expires: _____ , 20 _____   Notary Seal

State of _____
County of _____

On _____ , 20 _____ , _____ personally
came before me and, being duly sworn, did state that he or she is the person described in the
above document and that he or she signed the above document in my presence.

_____
Signature of Notary Public

Notary Public, In and for the County of _____
State of _____

My commission expires: _____ , 20 _____   Notary Seal

CHAPTER 7
Receipts

In this chapter, various receipt forms are provided. Receipts are a formal acknowledgment of having received something, whether it is money or property. For all of the following forms, the appropriate signature line from Chapter 4 should be used. Please note that three other receipt forms are included in this book in other chapters: Chapter 8 contains a Receipt for Lease Security Deposit and a Rent Receipt to be used in conjunction with leases of real estate; and Chapter 14 contains a Receipt for Collateral to be used in a business-financing situation.

Instructions

The following forms are included in this chapter:

Receipt in Full: This form should be used as a receipt for a payment which completely pays off a debt. You will need to include the amount paid, the name of the person who paid it, a description of the obligation which is paid off (for example: an invoice, statement, sales slip, note, or bill of sale), and the date when paid. The original receipt should go to the person making the payment, but a copy should be retained.

Receipt on Account: This form should be used as a receipt for a payment which does not fully pay off a debt, but, rather, is a payment on account and is credited to the total balance due. You will need to include the amount paid, the name of the person who paid it, a description of the account to which the payment is to be applied, and the date when paid. The original receipt should go to the person making the payment, but a copy should be retained.

Receipt for Goods: This form should be used as a receipt for the acceptance of goods. It is intended to be used in conjunction with a delivery order or purchase order. It also states that the goods have been inspected and found to be in conformance with the order. The original of this receipt should be retained by the person delivering the goods and a copy should go to the person accepting delivery.

Receipt in Full

The undersigned acknowledges receipt of the sum of $ _____ paid by
_____ .

This payment constitutes full payment and satisfaction of the following obligation:

Dated _____ , 20 _____

_____
Signature of Person Receiving Payment

_____
Printed Name of Person Receiving Payment

Receipt on Account

The undersigned acknowledges receipt of the sum of $ _____ paid by
_____ .

This payment will be applied and credited to the following account:

Dated _____ , 20 _____

_____
Signature of Person Receiving Payment

_____
Printed Name of Person Receiving Payment

Receipt for Goods

The undersigned acknowledges receipt of the goods which are described on the attached purchase order. The undersigned also acknowledges that these goods have been inspected and found to be in conformance with the purchase order specifications.

Dated _____ , 20 _____

_____
Signature of Person Receiving Goods

_____
Printed Name of Person Receiving Goods

CHAPTER 8

Leases of Real Estate

A *lease* of real estate is simply a written contract for one party to rent a specific property from another for a certain amount and certain time period. As such, all of the general legal ramifications that relate to contracts also relate to leases. However, all states have additional requirements which pertain only to leases. If the rental period is to be for one year or more, most states require that leases be in writing. Leases can be prepared for *periodic tenancies* (that is, for example, month-to-month or week-to-week) or they can be for a fixed period. The leases contained in this chapter provide for fixed-period tenancies.

There are also general guidelines for security deposits in most states. These most often follow a reasonable pattern and should be adhered to. Most states provide for the following with regard to lease security deposits:

- Should be no greater than one month's rent and should be fully refundable
- Should be used for the repair of damages only, and not applied for the nonpayment of rent (an additional month's rent may be requested to cover potential nonpayment of rent situations)
- Should be kept in a separate, interest-bearing account and returned, with interest, to the tenant within 10 days of termination of a lease (minus, of course, any deductions for damages)

In addition to state laws regarding security deposits, many states have requirements relating to the time periods required prior to terminating a lease. These rules have evolved over time to prevent both the landlord or the tenant from being harmed by early termination of a lease. In general, if the lease is for a fixed time period, the termination of the lease is governed by the lease itself. Early termination of a fixed-period lease may, however, be governed by individual state law. For periodic leases (month-to-month, etc.), there are normally state rules as to how much advance notice must be given prior to termination of a lease. If early lease termination is anticipated, check the state law regarding this issue.

Instructions

Residential Lease: This form should be used when renting a residential property. The following information will be necessary to prepare this form:

- The name and address of the landlord
- The name and address of the tenant

- A complete legal description of the leased property
- The length of time the lease will be in effect
- The amount of the rental payments
- The date of the month when the rent will be due
- The due date of the first rent payment
- The amount of the security deposit for damages
- The amount of additional rent held as rental default deposit
- Any utilities that the landlord will supply
- The utilities that the tenant will provide
- Landlord and tenant disclosures about lead-based paint and/or hazards
- Any other additional terms (for example, no pets)

Although the landlord and tenant can agree to any terms they desire, this particular lease provides for the following basic terms to be included:

- A fixed-period term for the lease
- A security deposit for damages, which will be returned within 10 days after the termination of the lease
- An additional month's rent as security for payment of the rent, which will be returned within 10 days after the termination of the lease
- That the tenant agrees to keep the property in good repair and not make any alterations without consent
- That the tenant agrees not to assign the lease or sublet the property without the landlord's consent
- That the landlord has the right to inspect the property on a reasonable basis, and that the tenant has already inspected it and found it satisfactory
- That the landlord has the right to re-enter and take possession upon breach of the lease (as long as it is in accordance with state law)
- That the landlord will provide tenant with the U.S. EPA lead pamphlet: "Protect Your Family from Lead in Your Home." *Note*: This document is provided on the Forms-on-CD and is necessary *only* if the rental dwelling was built prior to 1978
- Any other additional terms that the parties agree upon

Commercial Lease: This form should be used when renting a commercial property. The following information will be necessary to prepare this form:

- The name and address of the landlord
- The name and address of the tenant
- A complete legal description of the leased property
- The amount of square feet of interior space
- The length of time the lease will be in effect
- The amount of the rental payments

- The date of the month when the rent will be due
- The due date of the first rent payment
- The type of business that the tenant will operate on the property
- The amount of the security deposit for damages
- The amount of additional rent held as rental default deposit
- Any utilities that the landlord will supply
- The utilities that the tenant will provide
- Any equipment or fixtures that the tenant may install
- The amount of business liability insurance that the tenant agrees to keep in force during the term of the lease
- Any other additional terms (for example, no toxic chemicals)

Although the landlord and tenant can agree to any terms they desire, this particular lease provides for the following basic terms to be included:

- An initial fixed-period term for the lease, with the lease continuing on after this term as a month-to-month lease
- A five percent late charge for rent payments over five days late
- A limitation on what business the tenant may conduct on the property
- A security deposit for damages, which will be returned within 10 days after the termination of the lease
- An additional month's rent as security for payment of the rent, which will be returned within 10 days after the termination of the lease
- That the tenant agrees to keep the property in good repair and not make any alterations without consent
- That the tenant agrees not to assign the lease or sublet the property without the landlord's consent
- That the landlord has the right to inspect the property on a reasonable basis, and that the tenant has already inspected it and found it satisfactory
- That the landlord has the right to re-enter and take possession upon breach of the lease (as long as it is in accordance with state law)
- That the landlord is responsible for the upkeep of the exterior and the tenant for the upkeep of the interior of the property
- That the landlord will carry fire and casualty insurance on the property, and that the tenant will carry casualty insurance on their own equipment and fixtures and also carry general business liability insurance
- That the lease is subject to any mortgage or deed of trust and that the tenant agrees to sign any future subordination documents
- Any other additional terms that the parties agree upon

Assignment of Lease: This form is for use if one party to a lease is assigning its full interest in the lease to another party. This effectively substitutes one party for another under a lease. This particular assignment form has both of the parties agreeing to indemnify and hold each other harmless for any failures to perform under the lease while they were the party liable under it. This *indemnify and hold harmless* clause simply means that if a claim arises for failure to perform, each party agrees to be responsible for the period of their own performance obligations. A description of the lease which is assigned should include the parties to the lease, a description of the property, and the date of the lease. Other information that is necessary to complete the assignment is the name and address of the *assignor* (the party who is assigning the lease), the name and address of the *assignee* (the party to whom the lease is being assigned), and the date of the assignment. A copy of the original lease should be attached to this form. A copy of a Consent to Assignment of Lease should also be attached, if necessary.

Consent to Assignment of Lease: This form is used if the original lease states that the consent of the landlord is necessary for the assignment of the lease to be valid. A description of the lease and the name and signature of the person giving the consent are all that is necessary for completing this form. A copy of the original lease should be attached to this form.

Notice of Assignment of Lease: If a third party is involved in any of the obligations or benefits of an assigned lease, that party should be notified of the assignment in writing. This alerts the third party to look to the new party for satisfaction of any obligations under the lease or to make any payments under the lease directly to the new party. Use the following information to complete this form: a description of the lease, the names and addresses of the parties to the lease, and the effective date of the assignment of the lease. A copy of the original lease should be attached to this form. A copy of a Consent to Assignment of Lease should also be attached, if necessary.

Amendment of Lease: Use this form to modify any terms of a lease (for the expiration date, see next page). A copy of the original lease should be attached to this form. The amendment can be used to change any portion of the lease. Simply note what changes are being made in the appropriate place on this form. If a portion of the lease is being deleted, make note of the deletion. If certain language is being substituted, state the substitution clearly. If additional language is being added, make this clear. For example, you may wish to use language as follows:

- "Paragraph _____ is deleted from this lease."
- "Paragraph _____ is deleted from this lease and the following paragraph is substituted in its place:"
- "The following new paragraph is added to this lease:"

Extension of Lease: This document should be used to extend the effective time period during which a lease is in force. The use of this form allows the time limit to be extended without having to entirely re-draft the lease. Under this document, all of the other terms of the lease will remain the same, with only the expiration date changing.

You will need to fill in the original expiration date and the new expiration date. Other information necessary will be the names and addresses of the parties to the lease and a description of the lease. A copy of the original lease should be attached to this form.

Sublease: This form is used if the tenant subleases the property covered by an original lease. This particular sublease form has both of the parties agreeing to indemnify and hold each other harmless for any failures to perform under the lease while they were the party liable under it. This indemnify and hold harmless clause simply means that if a claim arises for failure to perform, each party agrees to be responsible for the period of their own performance obligations. A description of the lease which is subleased should include the parties to the lease, a description of the property, and the date of the lease. Use the following information to complete the sublease: the name and address of the original tenant, the name and address of the *subtenant* (the party to whom the property is being subleased), and the date of the sublease. A copy of the original lease should be attached to this form. A copy of a Consent to Sublease of Lease should also be attached, if necessary.

Consent to Sublease of Lease: This form is used if the original lease states that the consent of the landlord is necessary for a sublease to be valid. A description of the lease and the name and signature of the person giving the consent are all that is necessary for completing this form. A copy of the original lease should be attached to this form.

Notice of Breach of Lease: This form should be used to notify a party to a lease of the violation of a term of the lease or of an instance of failure to perform a required duty under the lease. It provides for a description of the alleged violation of the lease and for a time period in which the party is instructed to cure the breach of the lease. If the breach is not taken care of within the time period allowed, a lawyer should be consulted for further action, which may entail a lawsuit to enforce the lease terms. A copy of the original lease should be attached to this form.

Notice of Rent Default: This form allows for notice to a tenant of default in the payment of rent. It provides for the amount of the defaulted payments to be specified and for a time limit to be placed on payment before further action is taken. If the breach is not taken care of within the time period allowed, a lawyer should be consulted for further action, which may involve a lawsuit to enforce the lease terms. A copy of the original lease should be attached to this form.

Notice to Vacate Property: This notice informs a tenant who has already been notified of a breach of the lease (or of a defaulted rent payment) to vacate the property. It sets a specific date by which the tenant must be out of the property. If the tenant fails to leave by the date set, an attorney should be consulted to institute eviction proceedings.

Landlord's Notice to Terminate Lease: By this notice, a landlord may inform a tenant of the unilateral termination of a lease for breach of the lease. This action may be taken under the leases provided in this book because there are specific lease provisions that allow this action and (presumably) the tenant has agreed to these provisions. To complete this form, the lease should be described, the breach of the lease should be described, the date of the original Notice of Breach of Lease should be noted, and a date on which the tenant should deliver possession of the property to the landlord should be set.

Tenant's Notice to Terminate Lease: By this notice, a tenant may inform a landlord of the unilateral termination of a lease for breach of the lease. This action may be taken under the leases provided in this book because there are specific lease provisions that allow this action and (presumably) the landlord has agreed to these provisions. To complete this form, the lease should be described, the breach of the lease (reason for termination) should be described, and the date for delivery of possession back to the landlord should be set.

Mutual Termination of Lease: This form should be used when both the landlord and tenant desire to terminate a lease. To complete this form, simply fill in the names of the landlord and tenant and a description of the lease. This document releases both parties from any claims that the other may have against them for any actions under the lease. It also states that the landlord agrees that the rent has been paid in full and that the property has been delivered in good condition.

Receipt for Lease Security Deposit: This form is to be used for receipt of a lease security deposit. The amount of the deposit and a description of the leased property are all that is necessary for completion.

Rent Receipt: This form may be used as a receipt for the periodic payment of rent. It provides for the amount paid, the period paid for, and a description of the property.

Notice of Lease: This document should be used to record notice that a parcel of real estate has a current lease in effect on it. This may be necessary if the property is on the market for sale or it may be required by a bank or mortgage company. Requiring a notarization, this form may be completed with the following information:

- Name and address of the landlord and tenant
- Description of the property
- Term of the lease and any options to extend

Federal Lead Brochure: A text and full-color PDF-format copy of the U.S. EPA's pamphlet, "Protect Your Family from Lead in Your Home," is provided *only* on the included Forms-on-CD. A copy of this brochure must be provided to every potential buyer (or renter) of any residential dwelling that was built prior to 1978.

Residential Lease

This lease is made on _____ , 20 _____ , between
_____ , landlord,
address:

and _____ , tenant,
address:

1. The landlord agrees to rent to the tenant and the tenant agrees to rent from the landlord
    the following residence:

2. The term of this lease will be from _____ , 20 _____ , until
    _____ , 20 _____ .

3. The rental payments will be $ _____ per _____ and will
    be payable by the tenant to the landlord on the _____ day of each month,
    beginning on _____ , 20 _____ .

4. The tenant has paid the landlord a security deposit of $ _____ . This
    security deposit will be held as security for the repair of any damages to the residence by
    the tenant. This deposit will be returned to the tenant within ten (10) days of the termi-
    nation of this lease, minus any amounts needed to repair the residence.

5. The Tenant has paid the Landlord an additional month's rent in the amount of
    $ _____ . This rent deposit will be held as security for the payment
    of rent by the tenant. This rent payment deposit will be returned to the tenant within ten
    (10) days of the termination of this lease, minus any rent still due upon termination.

6. Tenant agrees to maintain the residence in a clean and sanitary manner and not to make
    any alterations to the residence without the landlord's written consent. Tenant also agrees
    not to conduct any business in the residence. At the termination of this lease, the tenant
    agrees to leave the residence in the same condition as when it was received, except for
    normal wear and tear.

7. The landlord agrees to supply the following utilities to the tenant:

8. The tenant agrees to obtain and pay for the following utilities:

9. Tenant agrees not to sublet the residence or assign this lease without the landlord's written consent. Tenant agrees to allow the landlord reasonable access to the residence for inspection and repair. Landlord agrees to enter the residence only after notifying the tenant in advance, except in an emergency.

10. The tenant has inspected the residence and has found it satisfactory.

11. If the tenant fails to pay the rent on time or violates any other terms of this lease, the landlord will have the right to terminate this lease in accordance with state law. The landlord will also have the right to re-enter the residence and take possession of it and to take advantage of any other legal remedies available.

12. As required by law, the landlord makes the following statement: "Radon gas is a naturally occurring radioactive gas that, when accumulated in sufficient quantities in a building, may present health risks to persons exposed to it. Levels of radon gas that exceed federal and state guidelines have been found in buildings in this state. Additional information regarding radon gas and radon gas testing may be obtained from your county health department."

13. As required by law, the landlord makes the following LEAD WARNING STATEMENT: "Every purchaser or lessee of any interest in residential real property on which a residential dwelling was built prior to 1978 is notified that such property may present exposure to lead from lead-based paint that may place young children at risk of developing lead poisoning. Lead poisoning in young children may produce permanent neurological damage, including learning disabilities, reduced intelligence quotient, behavioral problems, and impaired memory. Lead poisoning also poses a particular threat to pregnant women. The seller of any interest in residential real estate is required to provide the buyer with any information on lead-based paint hazards from risk assessments or inspection in the seller's possession and notify the buyer of any known lead-based paint hazards. A risk assessment or inspection for possible lead-based paint hazards is recommended prior to purchase."

Landlord's Disclosure

Presence of lead-based paint and/or lead-based paint hazards: (Landlord to initial one).

_____ Known lead-based paint and/or lead-based paint hazards are present in building (explain):

_____ Landlord has no knowledge of lead-based paint and/or lead-based paint hazards in building.

Records and reports available to landlord: (Landlord to initial one).

_____ Landlord has provided tenant with all available records and reports pertaining to lead-based paint and/or lead-based paint hazards are present in building (list documents):

_____ Landlord has no records and reports pertaining to lead-based paint and/or lead-based paint hazards in building.

Tenant's Acknowledgment

(Tenant to initial all applicable).

_____ Tenant has received copies of all information listed above.

_____ Tenant has received the pamphlet "Protect Your Family from Lead in Your Home."

_____ Tenant has received a ten (10)-day opportunity (or mutually agreed on period) to conduct a risk assessment or inspection for the presence of lead-based paint and/or lead-based paint hazards in building.

_____ Tenant has waived the opportunity to conduct a risk assessment or inspection for the presence of lead-based paint and/or lead-based paint hazards in building.

The landlord and tenant have reviewed the information above and certify, by their signatures at the end of this lease, to the best of their knowledge, that the information they have provided is true and accurate.

14. The following are additional terms of this lease:

15. The parties agree that this lease is the entire agreement between them. This lease binds and benefits both the landlord and tenant and any successors.

_____
Signature of Landlord

_____
Signature of Tenant

_____
Printed Name of Landlord

_____
Printed Name of Tenant

Commercial Lease

This lease is made on _____ , 20 _____ , between
_____ , landlord,
of _____ ,
City of _____ , State of _____ , and
_____ , tenant,
of _____ ,
City of _____ , State of _____ .

1. The landlord agrees to rent to the tenant and the tenant agrees to rent from the landlord the following commercial property:

   This property contains _____ square feet of interior floor space.

2. The term of this lease will be from _____ , 20 _____ , until _____ , 20 _____ . If the tenant continues to occupy the property, with the consent of the landlord, after the expiration of the original term of this lease, the rental will continue on a month-to-month basis with all of the other terms of this lease continuing unchanged.

3. The rental payments will be $ _____ per _____ and will be payable by the tenant to the landlord on the _____ day of each month, beginning on _____ , 20 _____ . If any rental payment is not paid within five (5) days of its due date, the tenant agrees to pay an additional late charge of five percent (5%) of the rental due.

4. The tenant agrees to use the property only for the purpose of carrying on the following business:

5. The tenant has paid the landlord a security deposit of $ _____ . This security deposit will be held as security for the repair of any damages to the property by the tenant. This deposit will be returned to the tenant within ten (10) days of the termination of this lease, minus any amounts needed to repair the property.

6. The tenant has paid the landlord an additional month's rent in the amount of $ _____ . This rent payment deposit will be held as security for the payment of rent by the tenant. This rent payment deposit will be returned to the tenant within ten (10) days of the termination of this lease, minus any rent still due upon termination.

7. The tenant agrees to maintain the property in a clean and sanitary manner and not to make any alterations to the property without the landlord's written consent. At the termination of this lease, the tenant agrees to leave the residence in the same condition as when it was received, except for normal wear and tear.

8. The landlord agrees to supply the following utilities to the tenant:

9. The tenant agrees to obtain and pay for the following utilities:

10. The tenant agrees not to sublet the property or assign this lease without the landlord's written consent. Tenant agrees to allow the landlord reasonable access to the property for inspection and repair. Landlord agrees to enter the property only after notifying the tenant in advance, except in an emergency.

11. The tenant has inspected the property and has found it satisfactory.

12. If the tenant fails to pay the rent on time or violates any other terms of this lease, the landlord will have the right to terminate this lease in accordance with state law. The landlord will also have the right to re-enter the residence and take possession of it and to take advantage of any other legal remedies available.

13. The landlord is responsible for the repair and upkeep of the exterior of the property and the tenant is responsible for the repair and upkeep of the interior of the property. The landlord agrees that the tenant may install the following equipment and fixtures for the purpose of operating the tenant's business:

14. The landlord agrees to carry fire and casualty insurance on the property, but does not have any liability for the operation of the tenant's business. The tenant agrees not to do anything that will increase the landlord's insurance premiums and, further, agrees to indemnify and hold the landlord harmless from any liability caused by tenant's operations. The tenant agrees to carry casualty insurance on any equipment or fixtures that tenant installs at the property. In addition, the tenant agrees to carry business liability insurance covering tenant's business operations in the amount of $ _____ with the landlord named as a co-insured party. Tenant agrees to furnish landlord copies of the insurance policies and to not cancel the policies without notifying the landlord in advance.

15. This lease is subject to any mortgage or deed of trust currently on the property or which may be made against the property at any time in the future. The tenant agrees to sign any documents necessary to subordinate this lease to a mortgage or deed of trust for the landlord.

16. The following are additional terms of this lease:

17. The parties agree that this lease is the entire agreement between them. This lease binds and benefits both the landlord and tenant and any successors.

_____
Signature of Landlord

_____
Printed Name of Landlord

_____
Signature of Tenant

_____
Printed Name of Tenant

106

Assignment of Lease

This assignment is made on _____ , 20 _____ , between
_____ , assignor,
address:

and _____ , assignee,
address:

For valuable consideration, the parties agree to the following terms and conditions:

1. The assignor assigns all interest, burdens, and benefits in the following described lease to the assignee:

This lease is attached to this assignment and is a part of this assignment.

2. The assignor warrants that this lease is in effect, has not been modified, and is fully assignable. If the consent of the landlord is necessary for this assignment to be effective, such consent is attached to this assignment and is a part of this assignment. Assignor agrees to indemnify and hold the assignee harmless from any claim which may result from the assignor's failure to perform under this lease prior to the date of this assignment.

3. The assignee agrees to perform all of the obligations of the assignor and receive all of the benefits of the assignor under this lease. Assignee agrees to indemnify and hold the assignor harmless from anyclaim which may result from the assignee's failure to perform under this lease after the date of this assignment.

4. This assignment binds and benefits both parties and any successors. This document, including any attachments, is the entire agreement between the parties.

_____   _____
Signature of Assignor   Signature of Assignee

_____   _____
Printed Name of Assignor   Printed Name of Assignee

Consent to Assignment of Lease

Date: _____ , 20 _____

To:_____ ,

RE: Assignment of Lease

Dear _____ :

I am the landlord under the following described lease:

This lease is the subject of the attached assignment of lease.

I consent to the assignment of this lease as described in the attached assignment, which pro-vides that the assignee is fully substituted for the assignor.

_____
Signature of Landlord

_____
Printed Name of Landlord

Notice of Assignment of Lease

Date: _____ , 20 _____

To: _____ ,

RE: Assignment of Lease

Dear _____ :

This notice is in reference to the following described lease:

Please be advised that as of _____ , 20 _____ , all interest and rights under this lease which were formerly owned by

_____
address:

have been permanently assigned to

_____
address:

Please be advised that all of the obligations and rights of the former party to this lease are now the responsibility of the new party to this lease.

_____
Signature of Assignor

_____
Printed Name of Assignor

Amendment of Lease

This amendment of lease is made on _____ , 20 _____ , between
_____ , landlord,
address:

and _____ , tenant,
address:

For valuable consideration, the parties agree as follows:

1. The following described lease is attached to this amendment and is made a part of this amendment:

2. The parties agree to amend this lease as follows:

3. All other terms and conditions of the original lease remain in effect without modification. This amendment binds and benefits both parties and any successors. This document, including the attached lease, is the entire agreement between the parties.

The parties have signed this amendment on the date specified at the beginning of this amendment.

_____   _____
Signature of Landlord   Signature of Tenant

_____   _____
Name of Landlord   Name of Tenant

Extension of Lease

This extension of lease is made on _____ , 20 _____ , between
_____ , landlord,
address:

and _____ , tenant,
address:

For valuable consideration, the parties agree as follows:

1. The following described lease will end on _____ , 20 _____ :

    This lease is attached to this extension and is a part of this extension.

2. The parties agree to extend this lease for an additional period, which will begin
    immediately on the expiration of the original time period and will end on
    _____ , 20 _____ .

3. The extension of this lease will be on the same terms and conditions as the original lease.
    This extension binds and benefits both parties and any successors. This document, includ-
    ing the attached lease, is the entire agreement between the parties.

The parties have signed this extension on the date specified at the beginning of this extension.

_____   _____
Signature of Landlord   Signature of Tenant

_____   _____
Printed Name of Landlord   Printed Name of Tenant

Sublease

This sublease is made on _____ , 20 _____ , between
_____ , tenant,
address:

and _____ , subtenant,
address:

For valuable consideration, the parties agree to the following terms and conditions:

1. The tenant subleases to the subtenant the following described property:

2. This property is currently leased to the tenant under the terms of the following described lease:

This lease is attached to this sublease and is a part of this sublease.

3. This sublease will be for the period from _____ , 20 _____ , to
_____ , 20 _____ .

4. The subrental payments will be $ _____ per _____ and will
be payable by the subtenant to the landlord on the _____ day of each month,
beginning on _____ , 20 _____ .

5. The tenant warrants that the underlying lease is in effect, has not been modified, and that the property may be sublet. If the consent of the landlord is necessary for his sublease to be effective, such consent is attached to this sublease and is a part of this sublease. Tenant agrees to indemnify and hold the subtenant harmless from any claim which may result from the tenant's failure to perform under this lease prior to the date of this sublease.

6. The subtenant agrees to perform all of the obligations of the tenant under the original lease and receive all of the benefits of the tenant under this lease. Subtenant agrees to indemnify and hold the tenant harmless from any claim which may result from the subtenant's failure to perform under this lease after the date of this sublease.

7. The tenant agrees to remain primarily liable to the landlord for the obligations under the lease.

8. The parties agree to the following additional terms:

9. This sublease binds and benefits both parties and any successors. This document, including any attachments, is the entire agreement between the parties.

_____   _____
Signature of Tenant   Signature of Subtenant

_____   _____
Printed Name of Tenant   Printed Name of Subtenant

Consent to Sublease of Lease

Date: _____ , 20 _____

To: _____ ,

RE: Sublease of Lease

Dear _____ :

I am the landlord under the following described lease:

This lease is the subject of the attached sublease.

I consent to the sublease of this lease as described in the attached sublease, which provides that the subtenant is substituted for the tenant for the period indicated in the sublease. This consent does not release the tenant from any obligations under the lease and the tenant remains fully bound under the lease.

_____
Signature of Landlord

_____
Printed Name of Landlord

Notice of Breach of Lease

Date: _____ , 20 _____

To: _____ ,

RE: Breach of Lease

Dear _____ :

This notice is in reference to the following described lease:

Please be advised that as of _____ , 20 _____ , we are holding you in BREACH OF LEASE for the following reasons:

If this breach of lease is not corrected within _____ days of this notice, we will take further action to protect our rights, which may include termination of this lease. This notice is made under all applicable laws. All of our rights are reserved under this notice.

_____
Signature of Landlord

_____
Printed Name of Landlord

Notice of Rent Default

Date: _____ , 20 _____

To: _____ ,

RE: Notice of Rent Default

Dear _____ :

This notice is in reference to the following described lease:

Please be advised that as of _____ , 20 _____ , you are in DEFAULT IN YOUR PAYMENT OF RENT in the amount of $ _____ .

If this breach of lease is not corrected within _____ days of this notice, we will take further action to protect our rights, which may include termination of this lease and collection proceedings. This notice is made under all applicable laws. All of our rights are reserved under this notice.

_____
Signature of Landlord

_____
Printed Name of Landlord

Notice to Vacate Property

Date: _____ , 20 _____

To: _____ ,

RE: Notice to Vacate Property

Dear _____ :

This notice is in reference to the following described lease:

Please be advised that since _____ , 20 _____ , you have been in BREACH OF LEASE for the following reasons:

You were previously notified of this breach in the NOTICE dated _____ , 20 _____ . At that time you were given _____ days to correct the breach of the lease and you have not complied.

THEREFORE, YOU ARE HEREBY GIVEN NOTICE:

To immediately vacate the property and deliver possession to the landlord on or before _____ , 20 _____ . If you fail to correct the breach of lease or vacate the property by this date, legal action to evict you from the property will be taken. Regardless of your vacating the property, you are still responsible for all rent due under the lease.

_____

Signature of Landlord

_____

Printed Name of Landlord

Landlord's Notice to Terminate Lease

Date: _____ , 20 _____

To: _____ ,

RE: Notice to Terminate Lease

Dear _____ :

This notice is in reference to the following described lease:

Please be advised that as of _____ , 20 _____ , you have been in BREACH OF LEASE for the following reasons:

You were previously notified of this breach in the NOTICE dated _____ , 20 _____ . At that time you were given _____ days to correct the breach of the lease and you have not complied.

THEREFORE, YOU ARE HEREBY GIVEN NOTICE:

The lease is immediately terminated and you are directed to deliver possession of the property to the landlord on or before _____ , 20 _____ . If you fail to deliver the property by this date, legal action to evict you from the property will be taken. Regardless of your deliverance of the property, you are still responsible for all rent due under the lease.

_____
Signature of Landlord

_____
Printed Name of Landlord

Tenant's Notice to Terminate Lease

Date: _____ , 20 _____

To: _____ ,

RE: Notice to Terminate Property

Dear _____ :

This notice is in reference to the following described lease:

Please be advised that as of _____ , 20 _____ , we are terminating the lease for the following reasons:

We intend to deliver possession of the property to the landlord on or before _____ , 20 _____ .

_____
Signature of Tenant

_____
Printed Name of Tenant

120

Mutual Termination of Lease

This termination of lease is made on _____ , 20 _____ , between
_____ , landlord,
address:

and _____ , tenant,
address:

For valuable consideration, the parties agree as follows:

1. The parties are currently bound under the terms of the following described lease:

2. They agree to mutually terminate and cancel this lease effective on this date. This termination agreement will act as a mutual release of all obligations under this lease for both parties, as if the lease has not been entered into in the first place. Landlord agrees that all rent due has been paid and that the possession of the property has been returned in satisfactory condition.

3. This termination binds and benefits both parties and any successors. This document, including the attached lease being terminated, is the entire agreement between the parties.

The parties have signed this termination on the date specified at the beginning of this termination.

_____   _____
Signature of Landlord   Signature of Tenant

_____   _____
Printed Name of Landlord   Printed Name of Tenant

Receipt for Lease Security Deposit

The landlord acknowledges receipt of the sum of $ _____ paid by the tenant under the following described lease:

This security deposit payment will be held by the landlord under the terms of this lease, and unless required by law, will not bear any interest. This security deposit will be repaid when due under the terms of the lease.

Dated: _____ , 20 _____

_____
Signature of Landlord

_____
Printed Name of Landlord

Rent Receipt

The landlord acknowledges receipt of the sum of $ _____ paid by _____ , the tenant, under the following described property:

Dated: _____ , 20 _____

_____
Signature of Landlord

_____
Printed Name of Landlord

Notice of Lease

NOTICE is given of the existence of the following lease:

Name of landlord:
address:

Name of tenant:
address:

Description of property leased:

Term of lease: From _____ , 20 _____ , to _____ , 20 _____ .

Any options to extend lease:

_____ _____
Signature   Printed Name

State of _____
County of _____

On _____ , 20 _____ , _____
personally came before me and, being duly sworn, did state that he or she is the person described in the above document and that he or she signed the above document in my presence.

_____
Signature of Notary Public

Notary Public, In and for the County of _____
State of _____

My commission expires: _____   Notary Seal

CHAPTER 9

Rental of Personal Property

Leases of personal property are often undertaken in the context of tools, equipment, or property necessary to perform a certain task. Other situations where such an agreement is often used is in the rental of property for recreational purposes. The needs of the parties to a personal property rental agreement depend a great deal on the type of property involved and the value of the property.

The two basic forms that are included in this chapter are somewhat at both ends of the spectrum with regard to rental of personal property. The first form is a very simple rental agreement that can be used for short-term rentals of relatively inexpensive property. The second form is a much more complex form that may be used for rentals of more valuable property. A personally tailored form may be constructed by adding particular clauses from the second form to the first form as the circumstances of a particular business situation dictate. Two termination of rental agreement forms are also included.

Instructions

Personal Property Rental Agreement (Simple): This form is designed to be used in situations involving inexpensive property for short terms. As you will see by comparing the clauses present in the second form (on page 125), this form does not address many of the potential problems that may arise in the rental of personal property. However, it does provide a legal basis for an enforceable contract between two parties regarding the rental of personal property.

The information necessary for the preparation of this form is simply the names and addresses of the parties (the "owner" and the "renter"), a description of the property, and the amount and term of the rental.

Personal Property Rental Agreement (Complex): This particular form is a far more detailed version of the basic rental agreement above. It is designed to be used in situations that call for more attention to potential problems relating to the rental. This generally means situations in which the property is more valuable.

This agreement addresses the following areas of concern:

- The inspection of the property by the renter and the renter's agreement to use the property in a careful manner
- A warranty by the owner that the property is safe and in good condition
- An indemnity agreement by the renter for damage to the property
- A disclaimer of liability by the owner
- Provisions for a security deposit to cover damages or late rental payments
- An agreement by the renter not to assign or transfer the property
- Responsibility for insuring the property
- Provisions for mediation and arbitration of disputes

The information necessary for filling in this form is as follows:

- The names and addresses of the parties (the owner and the renter)
- A description of the property
- The amount and term of the rental
- The amount of the security deposit
- The amount of insurance to be provided by the renter
- Any additional terms the parties desire
- The state whose laws will govern interpretation of the agreement

Renter's Notice to Terminate Rental Agreement: This form is to be used by the renter to provide the written notice required to terminate the complex personal property rental agreement. Simply fill in the name of the owner, a description of the rental agreement, and the date and reason for the termination.

Owner's Notice to Terminate Rental Agreement: This form is essentially identical to the above form, but is designed to be used by the owner (rather than the renter) to terminate the agreement. Fill in the name of the renter, a description of the rental agreement, and the date and reason for the termination.

Personal Property Rental Agreement (Simple)

This agreement is made on _____ , 20 _____ , between
_____ , owner,
address:

and _____ , renter,
address:

1. The owner agrees to rent to the renter and the renter agrees to rent from the owner the following property:

2. The term of this agreement will be from _____ o'clock ___ . m., _____ , 20 _____ , until _____ o'clock ___ . m., _____ , 20 _____ .

3. The rental payments will be $ _____ per _____ and will be payable by the renter to the owner as follows:

4. This agreement may be terminated by either party by giving twenty-four (24) hours notice to the other party.

5. The parties agree that this agreement is the entire agreement between them. This agreement binds and benefits both the owner and renter and any successors.

_____   _____
Signature of Owner   Signature of Renter

_____   _____
Printed Name of Owner   Printed Name of Renter

Personal Property Rental Agreement (Complex)

This agreement is made on _____ , 20 _____ , between
_____ , owner,
address:

and _____ , renter,
address:

1. The owner agrees to rent to the renter and the renter agrees to rent from the owner the following property:

2. The term of this agreement will be from _____ o'clock ___ . m.,
_____ , 20 _____ , until _____ o'clock ___ . m.
_____ , 20 _____ .

3. The rental payments will be $ _____ per _____ and will be payable by the renter to the owner as follows:

4. The renter agrees to pay a late fee of $ _____ per day that the rental payment is late. If the rental payments are in default for over _____ days, the owner may immediately demand possession of the property without advance notice to the renter.

5. The owner warrants that the property is free of any known faults which would affect its safe operation under normal usage and is in good working condition.

6. The renter states that the property has been inspected and is in good working condition. The renter agrees to use the property in a safe manner and in normal usage and to maintain the property in good repair. The renter further agrees not to use the property in a negligent manner or for any illegal purpose.

7. The renter agrees to fully indemnify the owner for any damage to or loss of the property during the term of this agreement, unless such loss or damage is caused by a defect of the rented property.

8. The owner shall not be liable for any injury, loss, or damage caused by any use of the property.

9. The renter has paid the owner a security deposit of $ _____ . This security deposit will be held as security for payments of the rent and for the repair of any damages to the property by the renter. This deposit will be returned to the renter upon the termination of this agreement, minus any rent still owed to the owner and minus any amounts needed to repair the property, beyond normal wear and tear.

10. The renter may not assign or transfer any rights under this agreement to any other person, nor allow the property to be used by any other person, without the written consent of owner.

11. Renter agrees to obtain insurance coverage for the property during the term of this rental agreement in the amount of $ _____ . Renter agrees to provide the owner with a copy of the insurance policy and to not cancel the policy during the term of this rental agreement.

12. This agreement may be terminated by either party by giving twenty-four (24) hours written notice to the other party.

13. Any dispute related to this agreement will be settled by voluntary mediation. If mediation is unsuccessful, the dispute will be settled by binding arbitration using an arbitrator of the American Arbitration Association.

14. The following are additional terms of this agreement:

15. The parties agree that this agreement is the entire agreement between them. This agreement binds and benefits both the owner and renter and any successors. Time is of the essence of this agreement.

16. This agreement is governed by the laws of the State of _____ .

_____   _____
Signature of Owner   Signature of Renter

_____   _____
Printed Name of Owner   Printed Name of Renter

Renter's Notice to Terminate Rental Agreement

Date: _____ , 20 _____

To: _____ ,

RE: Notice to Terminate Rental Agreement

Dear _____ :

This notice is in reference to the following described personal property rental agreement:

Please be advised that as of _____ , 20 _____ , we are terminating the personal property rental agreement for the following reasons:

We intend to deliver possession of the property to the owner on or before _____ , 20 _____ .

_____
Signature of Renter

_____
Printed Name of Renter

Owner's Notice to Terminate Rental Agreement

Date: _____ , 20 _____

To: _____ ,

RE: Notice to Terminate Rental Agreement

Dear _____ :

This notice is in reference to the following described personal property rental agreement:

Please be advised that as of _____ , 20 _____ , we are terminating the personal property rental agreement for the following reasons:

Please deliver possession of the property to the owner on or before _____ , 20 _____ .

_____
Signature of Owner

_____
Printed Name of Owner

CHAPTER 10

Sale of Personal Property

The forms in this chapter are for use when selling personal property. A contract for the sale of personal property may be part of a greater transaction (involving, for example, the sale of real estate or a complete business) or it may be prepared separate from any other dealings. A *bill of sale* provides a receipt for both parties that the sale has been consummated and the delivery of the item in question has taken place. Bills of sale are often utilized to document the sale of personal property that is part of a real estate transaction when the terms of the sale are part of the real estate sales contract.

Instructions

The following forms are provided in this section:

Contract for Sale of Personal Property: This form may be used for documenting the sale of any type of personal property. It may be used for vehicles, business assets, or any other personal property. To complete this form, fill in the names and addresses of the seller and the buyer, a complete description of the property being sold, the total purchase price, the terms of the payment of this price, and the date of possession.

Bill of Sale, with Warranties: This document is used as a receipt of the sale of personal property. It is, in many respects, often used to operate as a "title" to items of personal property. It verifies that the person noted in the bill of sale has obtained legal title to the property from the previous owner. This particular version also provides that the seller warrants that it has authority to transfer legal title to the buyer and that there are no outstanding debts or liabilities for the property. In addition, this form provides that the seller warrants that the property is in good working condition on the date of the sale. To complete this form, simply fill in the names and addresses of the seller and buyer, the purchase price of the item, and a description of the property.

Bill of Sale, without Warranties: This form also provides a receipt to the buyer for the purchase of an item of personal property. However, in this form, the seller makes no warranties at all, either regarding the authority to sell the item or the condition of the item. It is sold to the buyer in "as is" condition. The buyer takes it regardless of any defects. To complete this form, fill in the names and addresses of the seller and buyer, the purchase price of the item, and a description of the property.

Bill of Sale, Subject to Debt: This form also provides a receipt to the buyer for the purchase of an item of personal property. This form, however, provides that the property sold is subject to a certain prior debt. It verifies that the seller has obtained legal title to the property from the previous owner, but that the seller specifies that the property is sold subject to a certain debt which the buyer is to pay off. In addition, the buyer agrees to *indemnify* (reimburse or compensate) the seller regarding any liability on the debt. This particular version also provides that the seller warrants that he or she has authority to transfer legal title to the buyer. In addition, this form provides that the owner warrants that the property is in good working condition on the date of the sale. To complete this form, fill in the names and addresses of the seller and buyer, the purchase price of the item, a description of the property, and a description of the debt.

Contract for Sale of Personal Property

This contract is made on _____ , 20 _____ , between
_____ , seller,
address:

and _____ , buyer,
address:

1. The seller agrees to sell to the buyer, and the buyer agrees to buy the following personal property:

2. The buyer agrees to pay the seller $ _____ for the property. The buyer agrees to pay this purchase price in the following manner:

3. The buyer will be entitled to possession of this property on _____ , 20 _____ .

4. The seller represents that it has legal title to the property and full authority to sell the property. Seller also represents that the property is sold free and clear of all liens, indebtedness, or liabilities. Seller agrees to provide buyer with a bill of sale for the property.

5. This contract binds and benefits both the buyer and seller and any successors. This document, including any attachments, is the entire agreement between the buyer and seller. This agreement is governed by the laws of the State of _____ .

_____   _____
Signature of Seller   Signature of Buyer

_____   _____
Printed Name of Seller   Printed Name of Buyer

Bill of Sale, with Warranties

This bill of sale is made on _____ , 20 _____ , between
_____ , seller,
address:

and _____ , buyer,
address:

In exchange for the payment of $ _____ , received from the buyer, the seller sells and transfers possession of the following property to the buyer:

The seller warrants that it owns this property and that it has the authority to sell the property to the buyer. Seller also warrants that the property is sold free and clear of all liens, indebtedness, or liabilities.

The seller also warrants that the property is in good working condition as of this date.

Signed and delivered to the buyer on the above date.

_____   _____
Signature of Seller   Printed Name of Seller

Bill of Sale, without Warranties

This bill of sale is made on _____ , 20 _____ , between
_____ , seller,
address:

and _____ , buyer,
address:

In exchange for the payment of $ _____ , received from the buyer, the
seller sells and transfers possession of the following property to the buyer:

The seller disclaims any implied warranty of merchantability or fitness and the property is
sold in its present condition, "as is."

Signed and delivered to the buyer on the above date.

_____   _____
Signature of Seller   Printed Name of Seller

Bill of Sale, Subject to Debt

This bill of sale is made on _____ , 20 _____ , between
_____ , seller,
address:

and _____ , buyer,
address:

In exchange for the payment of $ _____ , received from the buyer, the seller sells and transfers possession of the following property to the buyer:

The seller warrants that it owns this property and that it has the authority to sell the property to the buyer. Seller also states that the property is sold subject to the following debt:

The buyer buys the property subject to the above debt and agrees to pay the debt. Buyer also agrees to indemnify and hold the seller harmless from any claim based on failure to pay off this debt.

The seller also warrants that the property is in good working condition as of this date.

Signed and delivered to the buyer on the above date.

_____   _____
Signature of Seller   Signature of Buyer

_____   _____
Printed Name of Seller   Printed Name of Buyer

CHAPTER 11

Sale of Real Estate

In this chapter are various forms for the sale and transfer of real estate. Although most real estate sales today are handled by real estate professionals, it is still perfectly legal to buy and sell property without the use of a real estate broker or lawyer. The forms provided in this chapter allow a businessperson to prepare the necessary forms for many basic real estate transactions. Please note, however, that there may be various state and local variations on sales contracts, mortgages, or other real estate documents. If in doubt, check with a local real estate professional or an attorney.

Instructions

The following forms are provided:

Agreement to Sell Real Estate: This form can be used for setting down an agreement to buy and sell property. It contains the basic clauses to cover situations that will arise in most typical real estate transaction. The following items are covered in this contract:

- That the sale is conditioned on the buyer being able to obtain financing 30 days prior to the closing
- That if the sale is not completed, the buyer will be given back the earnest money deposit, without interest or penalty
- That the seller will provide a Warranty Deed for the real estate and a Bill of Sale for any personal property included in the sale
- That certain items will be pro-rated and adjusted as of the closing date
- That the buyer and the seller may split the various closing costs
- That the seller represents that it has good title to the property and that the personal property included is in good working order
- That the title to the property will be evidenced by either title insurance or an abstract of title
- That the seller will provide the buyer with the U.S. EPA pamphlet: "Protect Your Family from Lead in Your Home." *Note*: This document is provided on the Forms-on-CD and is necessary *only* if the residential dwelling was built prior to 1978

In order to prepare this contract, the following information will be necessary:

- The names and addresses of the seller and buyer
- The address and description of the property involved
- The purchase price and terms of purchase of the property
  - A list of any personal property being sold
  - How the purchase price will be paid
  - The amount of the mortgage and number of monthly payments
  - The annual interest rate of the mortgage
  - The amount of earnest money paid on signing the contract
- The date, time, and place for closing the sale
- A list of documents for the buyer
- Which items will be adjusted and pro-rated at closing
- Which closing costs will be paid for by the seller and which by the buyer
- Whether there are any outstanding claims, liabilities, or indebtedness pertaining to the property
- Landlord and tenant disclosures about lead-based paint and/or hazards
- Whether there are any additional terms
- Which state's laws will be used to interpret the contract

Title insurance or an abstract of title will need to be obtained from a local title company or attorney. A Bill of Sale for any personal property (Chapter 10) and a Warranty Deed (page 149) will need to be prepared for use at the closing of the sale. Finally, a federal lead brochure will need to be provided to the buyer if the dwelling was built before 1978.

Option to Buy Real Estate Agreement: This form is designed to be used to offer an interested buyer a time period in which to have an exclusive option to purchase a parcel of real estate. It should be used in conjunction with a filled-in but unsigned copy of the above Agreement to Sell Real Estate. Through the use of this option agreement, the seller can offer the buyer a time during which he or she can consider the purchase without concern of a sale to another party.

This agreement provides that in exchange for a payment (which will be applied to the purchase price if the option is exercised), the buyer is given a period of time to accept the terms of a completed real estate contract. If the buyer accepts the terms and exercises the option in writing, the seller agrees to complete the sale. If the option is not exercised, the seller is then free to sell the property on the market and to retain the money paid for the option.

To complete this form, you will need the following information:

- The names and addresses of the seller and buyer
- The location and description of the property involved

- The amount of money to be paid for the option
- The time limit of the option
- The purchase price of the property
- Which state's laws will be used to interpret the contract

In addition, an Agreement to Sell Real Estate covering the property subject to the option to buy should be completed and attached to the option agreement. This contract will provide all of the essential terms of the actual agreement to sell the property.

Quitclaim Deed: Any transfers of real estate must be in writing. This type of deed is intended to be used when the seller is merely selling whatever interest he or she may have in the property. By using a quitclaim deed, a seller is not, in any way, guaranteeing that he or she actually owns any interest in the property. This type of deed may be used to settle any claims that a person may have to a piece of real estate, to settle disputes over property, or to transfer property between co-owners.

To prepare this deed, simply fill in the names and addresses of the *grantor* (the one selling the property) and the *grantee* (the one buying the property), and the legal description of the property. For this deed form to be recorded, it must be properly notarized.

Warranty Deed: This type of deed is used in most real estate situations. It provides that the seller is conveying to the buyer a full and complete title to the land without any restrictions or debts. If the property will be subject to any restrictions or debts, these should be noted in the legal description area provided.

To complete this deed, simply fill in the names and addresses of the grantor and the grantee, and the legal description of the property. For the transfer to actually take place, the grantor must give the actual deed to the grantee. In addition, in order for this document to be recorded, this form should be properly notarized.

Affidavit Of Title: This specialized type of affidavit is used in real estate transactions to verify certain information regarding a piece of property. An Affidavit of Title is often required by a mortgage lender prior to approving a mortgage. With an Affidavit of Title, a landowner or seller states, under oath, that he or she has full possession and ownership of the property being sold. The seller also states the existence of any liens or claims against the property and that he or she has full authority to sell the property.

The information necessary for filling in this form are the names and addresses of the seller and buyer of the property, a complete legal description of the property, and a description of any liens or claims against the property. This form should be notarized as it may be required to be recorded. If the person making the affirmed statement is acting in other than an individual capacity (such as the director of a corporation, for example), substitute the appropriate signature and acknowledgment forms from Chapter 4.

Deed of Trust: A deed of trust is a document that creates a security interest in a parcel of property. It is similar to a mortgage. It does not create the debt itself and so must be used in conjunction with a Promissory Note (from Chapter 15). Some states use mortgages for this purpose and some states entitle such documents "deeds of trust." The purpose of both is the same. This document must be notarized and recorded in the land records office of the county where the property is located in order to be effective. Because of the many local and state variations in these type of documents, this document is for informational purposes only. Please consult an attorney or real estate professional for information regarding preparation of a locally acceptable deed of trust.

Mortgage: A mortgage is also a document that creates a security interest in a parcel of property, similar to a deed of trust. It does not create the debt itself and so must be used in conjunction with a Promissory Note (from Chapter 15). Some states use mortgages for this purpose while other states refer to such documents as "deeds of trust." The purpose of both is the same: to create a security interest in the real estate. This document must be notarized and recorded in the land records office of the county where the property is located in order to be effective. Because of the many local and state variations in these type of documents, this document is provided here for informational purposes only. You are strongly advised to consult an attorney or real estate professional for information regarding preparation of a locally-acceptable mortgage.

Federal Lead Brochure: A text and full-color PDF-format copy of the U.S. EPA's pamphlet, "Protect Your Family from Lead in Your Home," is provided *only* on the included Forms-on-CD. A copy of this brochure must be provided to every potential buyer (or renter) of any residential dwelling that was built prior to 1978.

Agreement to Sell Real Estate

This agreement is made on _____ , 20 _____ , between
_____ , seller,
address:

and _____ , buyer,
address:

The seller now owns the following described real estate, located at
_____ ,
City of _____ , State of _____ .

For valuable consideration, the seller agrees to sell and the buyer agrees to buy this property for the following price and on the following terms:

1. The seller will sell this property to the buyer, free from all claims, liabilities, and indebtedness, unless noted in this agreement.

2. The following personal property is also included in this sale:

3. The buyer agrees to pay the seller the sum of $ _____ , which the seller agrees to accept as full payment. This agreement, however, is conditional upon the buyer being able to arrange suitable financing on the following terms at least thirty (30) days prior to the closing date for this agreement: A mortgage in the amount of $ _____ , payable in _____ monthly payments, with an annual interest rate of _____ % (_____ percent) .

4. The purchase price will be paid as follows:
   Earnest deposit .... $ _____
   Other deposit: .... $ _____
   Cash or certified check on closing .... $ _____
   (subject to any adjustments or prorations on closing)

   Total Purchase Price .... $ _____

5. The seller acknowledges receiving the earnest money deposit of $ _____
   from the buyer. If buyer fails to perform this agreement, the seller shall retain this money.
   If seller fails to perform this agreement, this money shall be returned to the buyer or the
   buyer may have the right of specific performance. If buyer is unable to obtain suitable
   financing at least thirty (30) days prior to closing, then this money will be returned to the
   buyer without penalty or interest.

6. This agreement will close on _____ , 20 _____ , at _____ o'clock
   ____ . m., at _____ ,
   City of _____ , State of _____ . At that time, and upon
   payment by the buyer of the portion of the purchase price then due, the seller will deliver
   to buyer the following documents:

   (a) A Bill of Sale for all personal property
   (b) A Warranty Deed for the real estate
   (c) A Seller's Affidavit of Title
   (d) A closing statement
   (e) Other documents:

7. At closing, pro-rated adjustments to the purchase price will be made for the following
   items:

   (a) Utilities
   (b) Property taxes
   (c) The following other items:

8. The following closing costs will be paid by the seller:

9. The following closing costs will be paid by the buyer:

10. Seller represents that it has good and marketable title to the property and will supply the buyer with either an abstract of title or a standard policy of title insurance. Seller further represents that the property is free and clear of any restrictions on transfer, claims, indebtedness, or liabilities except the following:

   (a) Zoning, restrictions, prohibitions, or requirements imposed by any governmental authority
   (b) Any restrictions appearing on the plat of record of the property
   (c) Public utility easements of record
   (d) Other:

   Seller warrants that there shall be no violations of zoning or building codes as of the date of closing. Seller also warrants that all personal property included in this sale will be delivered in working order on the date of closing.

11. At least thirty (30) days prior to closing, buyer shall have the right to obtain a written report from a licensed termite inspector stating that there is no termite infestation or termite damage to the property. If there is such evidence, seller shall remedy such infestation and/or repair such damage, up to a maximum cost of two (2) percent of the purchase price of the property. If the costs exceed two (2) percent of the purchase price and seller elects not to pay for the costs over two (2) percent, buyer may cancel this agreement and the escrow shall be returned to buyer without penalty or interest.

12. At least thirty (30) days prior to closing, buyer or their agent shall have the right to inspect all heating, air conditioning, electrical, and mechanical systems of the property, the roof and all structural components of the property, and any personal property included in this agreement. If any such systems or equipment are not in working order, seller shall pay for the cost of placing them in working order prior to closing. Buyer or their agent may again inspect the property withing forty-eight (48) hours of closing to determine if all systems and equipment are in working order.

13. Between the date of this agreement and the date for closing, the property shall be maintained in the condition as existed on the date of this agreement. If there is any damage by fire, casualty, or otherwise, prior to closing, seller shall restore the property to the condition as existed on the date of this agreement. If seller fails to do so, buyer may:

(a) accept the property, as is, along with any insurance proceeds due seller, *or*

(b) cancel this agreement and have the escrow deposit returned, without penalty or interest.

14. As required by law, the seller makes the following statement: "Radon gas is a naturally occurring radioactive gas that, when accumulated in sufficient quantities in a building, may present health risks to persons exposed to it. Levels of radon gas that exceed federal and state guidelines have been found in buildings in this state. Additional information regarding radon gas and radon gas testing may be obtained from your county health department."

15. As required by law, the seller makes the following *Lead Warning Statement*: "Every purchaser of any interest in residential real property on which a residential dwelling was built prior to 1978 is notified that such property may present exposure to lead from lead-based paint that may place young children at risk of developing lead poisoning. Lead poisoning in young children may produce permanent neurological damage, including learning disabilities, reduced intelligence quotient, behavioral problems, and impaired memory. Lead poisoning also poses a particular threat to pregnant women. The seller of any interest in residential real estate is required to provide the buyer with any information on lead-based paint hazards from risk assessments or inspection in the seller's possession and notify the buyer of any known lead-based paint hazards. A risk assessment or inspection for possible lead-based paint hazards is recommended prior to purchase."

Seller's Disclosure

Presence of lead-based paint and/or lead-based paint hazards: (Seller to initial one).

_____ Known lead-based paint and/or lead-based paint hazards are present in building (explain):

_____ Seller has no knowledge of lead-based paint and/or lead-based paint hazards in building.

Records and reports available to seller: (Seller to initial one).

_____ Seller has provided buyer with all available records and reports pertaining to lead-based paint and/or lead-based paint hazards are present in building (list documents):

_____ Seller has no records and reports pertaining to lead-based paint and/or lead-based paint hazards in building.

Buyer's Acknowledgment

(Buyer to initial all applicable).

_____ Buyer has received copies of all information listed above.

_____ Buyer has received the pamphlet "Protect Your Family From Lead in Your Home."

_____ Buyer has received a ten (10)-day opportunity (or mutually agreed-on period) to conduct a risk assessment or inspection for the presence of lead-based paint and/or lead-based paint hazards in building.

_____ Buyer has waived the opportunity to conduct a risk assessment or inspection for the presence of lead-based paint and/or lead-based paint hazards in building.

The seller and buyer have reviewed the information above and certify, by their signatures at the end of this agreement, that to the best of their knowledge, the information they have provided is true and accurate.

16. The parties also agree to the following additional terms:

17. No modification of this agreement will be effective unless it is in writing and is signed by both the buyer and seller. This agreement binds and benefits both the buyer and seller and any successors. Time is of the essence of this agreement. This document, including any attachments, is the entire agreement between the buyer and seller. This agreement is governed by the laws of the State of _____ .

_____
Signature of Seller

_____
Printed Name of Seller

_____
Signature of Witness for Seller

_____
Printed Name of Witness for Seller

_____
Signature of Witness for Seller

_____
Printed Name of Witness for Seller

_____
Signature of Buyer

_____
Printed Name of Buyer

_____
Signature of Witness for Buyer

_____
Printed Name of Witness for Buyer

_____
Signature of Witness for Buyer

_____
Printed Name of Witness for Buyer

Option to Buy Real Estate Agreement

This agreement is made on _____ , 20 _____ , between

_____ , seller,

address:

and _____ , buyer,

address:

The seller now owns the following described real estate, located at

_____ ,

City of _____ , State of _____ .

For valuable consideration, the seller agrees to give the buyer an exclusive option to buy this property for the following price and on the following terms:

1. The buyer will pay the seller $ _____ for this option. This amount will be credited against the purchase price of the property if this option is exercised by the buyer. If the option is not exercised, the seller will retain this payment.

2. The option period will be from the date of this agreement until _____ , 20 _____ , at which time it will expire unless exercised.

3. During this period, the buyer has the option and exclusive right to buy the seller's property mentioned above for the purchase price of $ _____ . The buyer must notify the seller, in writing, of the decision to exercise this option.

4. Attached to this option agreement is a completed contract for the sale of real estate. If the buyer notifies the seller, in writing, of the decision to exercise the option within the option period, the seller and buyer agree to sign the contract for the sale of real estate and complete the sale on the terms contained in the contract.

5. No modification of this agreement will be effective unless it is in writing and is signed by both the buyer and seller. This agreement binds and benefits both the buyer and seller and any successors. Time is of the essence of this agreement. This document, including any attachments, is the entire agreement between the buyer and seller. This agreement is governed by the laws of the State of _____ .

_____   _____

Signature of Seller   Printed Name of Seller

_____   _____

Signature of Buyer   Printed Name of Buyer

Quitclaim Deed

This Quitclaim Deed is made on _____ , 20 _____ , between
_____ , grantor,
address:

and _____ , grantee,
address:

For valuable consideration, the grantor hereby quitclaims and transfers the following described real estate to the grantee to have and hold forever, located at
_____ ,
City of _____ , State of _____ .

Dated: _____ , 20 _____

_____   _____
Signature of Grantor   Printed Name of Grantor

State of _____
County of _____

On _____ , 20 _____ , _____ personally
came before me and, being duly sworn, did state that he or she is the person described in the above document and that he or she signed the above document in my presence.

_____
Signature of Notary Public

Notary Public, In and for the County of _____
State of _____

My commission expires: _____   Notary Seal

Warranty Deed

This warranty deed is made on _____ , 20 _____ , between
_____ , grantor,
address:

and _____ , grantee,
address:

For valuable consideration, the grantor hereby sells, grants, and conveys the following described real estate, in fee simple, to the grantee to have and hold forever, along with all easements, rights, and buildings belonging to the above property, located at

_____ ,
City of _____ , State of _____ .

The Grantor warrants that it is lawful owner and has full right to convey the property, and that the property is free from all claims, liabilities, or indebtedness, and that the Grantor and its successors will warrant and defend title to the Grantee against the lawful claims of all persons.

Dated: _____ , 20 _____

_____   _____
Signature of Grantor   Printed Name of Grantor

State of _____
County of _____

On _____ , 20 _____ , _____ personally came before me and, being duly sworn, did state that he or she is the person described in the above document and that he or she signed the above document in my presence.

_____
Signature of Notary Public

Notary Public, In and for the County of _____
State of _____

My commission expires: _____   Notary Seal

Affidavit of Title

This affidavit of title is made on _____ , 20 _____ , between
_____ , seller,
address:

for _____ , buyer,
address:

1. Seller certifies that it is now in possession of and is the absolute owner of the following property:

2. Seller also states that its possession has been undisputed and that seller knows of no fact or reason that may prevent transfer of this property to the buyer.

3. Seller also states that no liens, contracts, debts, or lawsuits exist regarding this property, except the following:

4. Seller finally states that it has full power to transfer full title to this property to the buyer.

Dated: _____ , 20 _____

_____   _____
Signature of Seller   Printed Name of Seller

State of _____
County of _____

On _____ , 20 _____ , _____ personally
came before me and, being duly sworn, did state that he or she is the person described in the above document and that he or she signed the above document in my presence.

_____
Signature of Notary Public

Notary Public, In and for the County of _____
State of _____

My commission expires: _____   Notary Seal

150

Deed of Trust

This deed of trust is made on _____ , 20 _____ , between
_____ , grantor,
address:

and _____ , grantee,
address:

1. For valuable consideration, the grantor hereby grants the following described real estate
    to the trustee in TRUST, along with all easements, rights, and buildings belonging to the
    above property, located at

    _____ ,
    City of _____ , State of _____ .

2. This property is granted in TRUST to the trustee to secure payment of the balance of the
    purchase price for the property owed to the grantor by

    _____ , grantee,
    address:

3. The balance of the purchase price for this property is evidenced by a promissory note dated
    _____ , 20 _____ , in the principal amount of $ _____ ,
    which is payable on or before _____ , 20 _____ , and bears interest
    at the annual rate of _____ % (_____ percent), and which is payable
    to _____ ,
    address:

    A copy of the promissory note is attached and all of the terms of the note are made part
    of this document.

4. Upon evidence of full payment of the Promissory Note and satisfaction of all of the terms of the note, the Trustee shall deliver a signed Deed of Release to the Grantee.

Dated: _____ , 20 _____

_____   _____
Signature of Grantor   Printed Name of Grantor

State of _____
County of _____

On _____ , 20 _____ , _____ personally came before me and, being duly sworn, did state that he or she is the person described in the above document and that he or she signed the above document in my presence.

_____
Signature of Notary Public

Notary Public, In and for the County of _____
State of _____

My commission expires: _____   Notary Seal

Mortgage

This mortgage is made on _____ , 20 _____ , between
_____ , mortgagor,
address:

and _____ , mortgagee,
address:

1. For valuable consideration, the mortgagor hereby mortgages, grants, and conveys the following described real estate, in fee simple, to the mortgagee to have and hold forever, along with all easements, rights, and buildings belonging to the above property, located at _____ ,
City of _____ , State of _____ :

2. This property is granted as security to the mortgagee to secure payment of the balance of the purchase price for the property which is owed to the mortgagee by the mortgagor.

3. The balance of the purchase price for this property is evidenced by a promissory note dated _____ , 20 _____ , in the principal amount of $ _____ , which is payable on or before _____ , 20 _____ , and bears interest at the annual rate of _____ % (_____ percent), and which is payable to mortgagee. A copy of the promissory note is attached and all of the terms of the note are made part of this document.

4. Upon evidence of full payment of the promissory note and satisfaction of all of the terms of the note, the mortgagee agrees to deliver a signed release of this mortgage to the mortgagor.

5. The mortgagor warrants that he or she is lawful owner and has full right to convey the property, and that the property is free from all claims, liabilities, or indebtedness, and that the mortgagor, and his or her successors will warrant and defend title to the mortgagee against the lawful claims of all persons.

Dated: _____ , 20 _____

_____
Signature of Mortgagor

_____
Printed Name of Mortgagor

State of _____
County of _____

On _____ , 20 _____ , _____ personally came before me and, being duly sworn, did state that he or she is the person described in the above document and that he or she signed the above document in my presence.

_____
Signature of Notary Public

Notary Public, In and for the County of _____
State of _____

My commission expires: _____

Notary Seal

CHAPTER 12

Employment Documents

The legal forms in this section cover a variety of situations that arise in the area of employment. From hiring an employee to subcontracting work on a job, written documents which outline the party's responsibilities and duties are important for keeping an employment situation on an even keel. The employment contract contained in this chapter may be used and adapted for virtually any employment situation. Of course, it is perfectly legal to hire an employee without a contract at all. In many businesses, this is common practice. However, as job skills and salaries rise and employees are allowed access to sensitive and confidential business information, written employment contracts are often prudent business practice. An *independent contractor* may also be hired to perform a job. As opposed to an *employee*, these types of worker maintain their own independent business, use their own tools, and do not work under the direct supervision of the person who has hired them. A contract for hiring an independent contractor is provided in this chapter.

Instructions

General Employment Contract: May be used for any situation where an employee is hired for a specific job. The issues addressed by this contract are that the employee:

- Will perform a certain job and any incidental further duties
- Will be hired for a certain period and for a certain salary
- Will be given certain job benefits (for example, sick pay, vacations, etc.)
- Agrees to abide by the employer's rules and regulations
- Agrees to sign agreements regarding confidentiality and inventions
- Agrees to submit any employment disputes to mediation and arbitration

The information necessary to complete this form is as follows:

- The names and addresses of the employer and employee
- A complete description of the job
- The date the job is to begin and the length of time that the job will last
- The amount of compensation and benefits for the employee
- Terms for termination
- List of additional documents for employee to sign
- Any additional terms
- The state whose laws will govern the contract

Employee Confidentiality Agreement: This form may be used in those situations in which it is prudent to have the employee agree not to divulge any business or trade secrets. An employer's business secrets include any information regarding the employer's customers, supplies, finances, research, development or manufacturing processes, or any technical or business information. This form also provides that the employee agrees not to make any unauthorized copies of information or take any business information from the employer's facilities. To prepare this form, simply fill in the employer's and employee's names and addresses and any additional terms.

Employee Patents and Inventions Agreement: This form is for use in those situations in which a dispute may arise over who owns an invention which an employee created while on the job for an employer. By using this form, the employee agrees to provide the employer with any information about such an invention. In addition, this document serves as an assignment and transfer to the employer of any rights that the employee may have had in any invention created on the job. To prepare this form, simply fill in the employer's and employee's names and addresses and any additional terms.

Consent to Release Employment Information: This form is used to obtain an employee's consent to have a previous employer release past job records regarding the employee. This form may be completed by supplying the employee's name and address, the current employer's name and address, and the former employer's name and address.

Independent Contractor Agreement: This form should be used when hiring an independent contractor. It provides a standard form for the hiring out of specific work to be performed within a set time-period for a particular payment. It also provides a method for authorizing extra work under the contract. Finally, this document provides that the contractor agrees to indemnify the owner against any claims or liabilities arising from the performance of the work. To complete this form, fill in the names and addresses of the owner and contractor, a detailed description of the work, dates by which portions of the job are to be completed, the pay for the job, the terms and dates of payment, and the state whose laws will govern the contract.

Contractor/Subcontractor Agreement: This form is intended to be used by an independent contractor to hire a subcontractor to perform certain work on a job that the contractor has agreed to perform. It provides for the "farming" out of specific work to be performed by the subcontractor within a set-time period for a particular payment. It also provides a method for authorizing extra work under the contract. Finally, this document provides that the subcontractor agrees to indemnify the contractor against any claims or liabilities arising from the performance of the work. To complete this form, fill in the names and addresses of the contractor and subcontractor, the date of the original contractor agreement, a detailed description of the work, dates by which portions of the job are to be completed, the pay for the job, the terms and dates of payment, and the state whose laws will govern the contract.

General Employment Contract

This contract is made on _____ , 20 _____ , between
_____ , employer, of
_____ , City of _____ ,
State of _____ , and _____ ,
employee, of _____ , City of
_____ , State of _____ .

For valuable consideration, the employer and employee agree as follows:

1. The employee agrees to perform the following duties and job description:

The employee also agrees to perform further duties incidental to the general job description. This is considered a full-time position.

2. The employee will begin work on _____ , 20 _____ . This position shall continue for a period of _____ .

3. The employee will be paid the following:

   Weekly salary: $ _____

The employee will also be given the following benefits:

   Sick pay: $ _____
   Vacations: $ _____
   Bonuses: $ _____
   Retirement benefits: $ _____
   Insurance benefits: $ _____

4. The employee agrees to abide by all rules and regulations of the employer at all times while employed.

5. This contract may be terminated by:

   (a) Breach of this contract by the employee
   (b) The expiration of this contract without renewal
   (c) Death of the employee
   (d) Incapacitation of the employee for over _____ days in any one (1) year

6. The employee agrees to sign the following additional documents as a condition to obtaining employment:

7. Any dispute between the employer and employee related to this contract will be settled by voluntary mediation. If mediation is unsuccessful, the dispute will be settled by binding arbitration using an arbitrator of the American Arbitration Association.

8. Any additional terms of this contract:

9. No modification of this contract will be effective unless it is in writing and is signed by both the employer and employee. This contract binds and benefits both parties and any successors. Time is of the essence of this contract. This document is the entire agreement between the parties. This contract is governed by the laws of the State of _____ .

Dated: _____ , 20 _____

_____   _____
Signature of Employer   Signature of Employee

_____   _____
Printed Name of Employer   Printed Name of Employee

Employee Confidentiality Agreement

This agreement is made on _____ , 20 _____ , between
_____ , employer, of
_____ ,
City of _____ , State of _____ , and
_____ , employee, of
_____ ,
City of _____ , State of _____ .

For valuable consideration, the employer and employee agree as follows:

1. The employee agrees to keep all of the employer's business secrets confidential at all times during and after the term of employee's employment. Employer's business secrets include any information regarding the employer's customers, supplies, finances, research, development, manufacturing processes, or any other technical or business information.

2. The employee agrees not to make any unauthorized copies of any of employer's business secrets or information without employer's consent, nor to remove any of employer's business secrets or information from the employer's facilities.

3. The parties agree to the following additional terms:

Dated: _____ , 20 _____

_____
Signature of Employer

_____
Printed Name of Employer

_____
Signature of Employee

_____
Printed Name of Employee

Employee Patents and Inventions Agreement

This agreement is made on _____ , 20 _____ , between
_____ , employer, of
_____ ,
City of _____ , State of _____ , and
_____ , employee, of
_____ ,
City of _____ , State of _____ .

For valuable consideration, the employer and employee agree as follows:

1. The employee agrees to promptly furnish the employer with a complete record of any inventions or patents which the employee may create or devise during employment with the employer.

2. The employee grants and assigns to the employer her or his entire rights and interest in any inventions or patents that result in any way from any work performed while employed by the employer. The employee agrees that he or she does not have any past employment agreements, patents, or inventions that might conflict with this assignment. The employer also agrees to sign any further documents necessary to allow the employer the rights, title, or patent to any such inventions or creations.

3. The parties agree to the following additional terms:

Dated: _____ , 20 _____

_____
Signature of Employer

_____
Signature of Employee

_____
Printed Name of Employer

_____
Printed Name of Employee

Consent to Release
Employment Information

I, _____ , of

_____ ,

City of _____ , State of _____ , do consent and authorize

_____ , of

_____ ,

City of _____ , State of _____ , to release any and all
employment records of mine that they might have in their possession to

_____ , of

_____ ,

City of _____ , State of _____ .

I release the above party from any liability for the release of any information or records based
on this consent and authorization.

Dated: _____ , 20 _____

_____
Signature of Employee

_____
Printed Name of Employee

Independent Contractor Agreement

This agreement is made on _____ , 20 _____ , between
_____ , owner, of
_____ ,
City of _____ , State of _____ , and
_____ , contractor, of
_____ ,
City of _____ , State of _____ .

For valuable consideration, the owner and contractor agree as follows:

1. The contractor agrees to furnish all of the labor and materials to do the following work for the owner as an independent contractor:

2. The contractor agrees that the following portions of the total work will be completed by the dates specified:

162

3. The contractor agrees to perform this work in a workmanlike manner according to standard practices. If any plans or specifications are part of this job, they are attached to and are part of this agreement.

4. The owner agrees to pay the contractor as full payment $ _____ , for doing the work outlined above. This price will be paid to the contractor on satisfactory completion of the work in the following manner and on the following dates:

5. The contractor and the owner may agree to extra services and work, but any such extras must be set out and agreed to in writing by both the contractor and the owner.

6. The contractor agrees to indemnify and hold the owner harmless from any claims or liability arising from the contractor's work under this agreement.

7. No modification of this agreement will be effective unless it is in writing and is signed by both parties. This agreement binds and benefits both parties and any successors. Time is of the essence of this agreement. This document, including any attachments, is the entire agreement between the parties. This agreement is governed by the laws of the State of _____ .

Dated: _____ , 20 _____

_____
Signature of Owner

_____
Printed Name of Owner

_____
Signature of Contractor

_____
Printed Name of Contractor

Contractor/Subcontractor Agreement

This agreement is made on _____ , 20 _____ , between
_____ , contractor, of
_____ ,

City of _____ , State of _____ , and
_____ , subcontractor, of
_____ ,

City of _____ , State of _____ .

1. The subcontractor, as an independent contractor, agrees to furnish all of the labor and materials to do the following portions of the work specified in the agreement between the contractor and the owner dated _____ , 20 _____ :

2. The subcontractor agrees that the following portions of the total work will be completed by the dates specified:

3. The subcontractor agrees to perform this work in a workmanlike manner according to standard practices. If any plans or specifications are part of this job, they are attached to and are part of this agreement.

4. The contractor agrees to pay the subcontractor as full payment $ _____ , for doing the work outlined above. This price will be paid to the subcontractor on satisfactory completion of the work in the following manner and on the following dates:

5. The contractor and subcontractor may agree to extra services and work, but any such extras must be set out and agreed to in writing by both the contractor and the subcontractor.

6. The subcontractor agrees to indemnify and hold the contractor harmless from any claims or liability arising from the subcontractor's work under this agreement.

7. No modification of this agreement will be effective unless it is in writing and is signed by both parties. This agreement binds and benefits both parties and any successors. Time is of the essence of this agreement. This document, including any attachments, is the entire agreement between the parties. This agreement is governed by the laws of the State of _____ .

Dated: _____ , 20 _____

_____
Signature of Contractor

_____
Printed Name of Contractor

_____
Signature of Subcontractor

_____
Printed Name of Subcontractor

CHAPTER 13
Business Credit Documents

The forms that are contained in this chapter relate to the extension of business credit to customers. In many business situations it is customary to offer credit to continuing customers on mutually agreeable terms. The prudent businessperson, however, should take certain steps to assure that the company that is being offered credit is a sound business risk. The various forms provided allow for the collection of credit information and for the evaluation of the credit potential of business customers.

Instructions

Business Credit Application: This form is the basis of a check into the credit history of a customer. With this form a company desiring credit furnishes various information which may be checked further to ascertain the reliability and background of the credit applicant.

The credit applicant is requested to furnish the following information:

- Company name and address
- Type of business
- Length of time in business
- Gross annual sales, net profits, and net value of the company
- Names and addresses of owners, partners, or officers of the company
- Credit references
- Trade references
- Bank references

In addition, the applicant is asked to request a credit limit for his or her account. Finally, the various credit terms that are being applied for are spelled out. The following information will need to be filled in before sending the form to a potential credit customer: the interest rate on overdue balances and number of days within which an invoice is to be paid.

Notice of Approval of Business Credit Application: This form is used to approve the above credit application. It should be sent only after the information in the credit application has been thoroughly checked and approved. This form reiterates the credit terms that your company is offering to the applicant.

166

Request for Bank Credit Reference: This form is intended to be used to contact the various banking references that a credit applicant has offered in his or her Business Credit Application. It requests the bank to provide confidential information regarding the applicant's banking and credit history with the bank. A copy of the applicant's Business Credit Application should be attached to this request when sending it to the bank.

Request for Trade Credit Reference: This form is intended to be used to contact the various trade references that a credit applicant has offered in his or her Business Credit Application. It requests that the trade vendor provide confidential information regarding the applicant's banking and credit history with the vendor. A copy of the applicant's Business Credit Application should be attached to this request when sending it to the vendor.

Request for Credit Information: This final form is designed to be used to obtain information regarding your personal credit history from any credit reporting agency. It is in accordance with the Federal Fair Credit Reporting Act. Fill in the appropriate information and forward it to the credit reporting agency from which you wish to obtain information.

Business Credit Application

Company Name _____
Billing Address:

Phone _____
Fax _____
Telex _____
Email Address _____

___ Corporation   ___ Partnership   ___ Proprietorship   ___ Other
If other, explain _____
Type of Business _____   Year Established _____

Yearly Gross Sales $ _____
Yearly Net Profits $ _____
Net Value $ _____

Names and Addresses of Owners, Partners, or Officers

Name _____
SS# _____   Title _____
Address:

Name _____
SS# _____   Title _____
Address:

Name _____
SS# _____   Title _____
Address:

Name _____
SS# _____   Title _____
Address:

Credit References

Creditor Name _____
Account # _____ Phone _____
Address:

Creditor Name _____
Account # _____ Phone _____
Address:

Creditor Name _____
Account # _____ Phone _____
Address:

Creditor Name _____
Account # _____ Phone _____
Address:

Trade Credit References

Vendor Name _____
Account # _____ Phone _____
Address:

Vendor Name _____
Account # _____ Phone _____
Address:

Vendor Name _____
Account # _____ Phone _____
Address:

Vendor Name _____
Account # _____ Phone _____
Address:

Bank References

Bank Name _____
Account # _____ Phone _____
Address:

Bank Name _____
Account # _____ Phone _____
Address:

Bank Name _____
Account # _____ Phone _____
Address:

CREDIT LIMIT REQUESTED: $ _____

Credit Terms

- Payment on all invoices is due within _____ days of invoice date.
- All overdue invoices bear interest at _____ % (_____ percent) per month on unpaid balance.
- Credit applicant agrees to pay all costs of collection, including court costs and attorneys fees.
- Credit terms and limit may be cancelled or changed by Creditor at any time without notice.
- All transactions are governed by the laws of the Creditor's state.
- All transactions are governed by the terms of the Creditor's documents.

The credit applicant accepts the above terms and states that all information contained in this credit application is true and correct. Credit applicant authorizes creditor to contact all references, inquire as to credit information, and receive any confidential information relevant to approving credit.

Dated: _____ , 20 _____

_____   _____
Signature of Credit Applicant   Printed Name of Credit Applicant

Notice of Approval of
Business Credit Application

Date: _____ , 20 _____

To: _____

RE: Credit Application

Dear _____

Please be advised that, based upon your credit application which you filed with our firm dated _____ , 20 _____ , your credit has been approved.

Please be further advised that your initial credit limit is $ _____ .

The terms of this extension of credit to your company are as follows:

- Payment on all invoices is due within _____ days of invoice date.
- All overdue invoices bear interest at _____ % (_____ percent) per month on unpaid balance.
- Credit applicant agrees to pay all costs of collection, including court costs and attorneys fees.
- Credit terms and limit may be cancelled or changed by creditor at any time without notice.
- All transactions are governed by the laws of the creditor's state.
- All transactions are governed by the terms of the creditor's documents.

If you have any questions regarding this matter, please contact our accounting department. Thank you very much and we look forward to doing business with you.

Very truly,

_____
Signature

_____
Printed Name

Request for Bank Credit Reference

Date: _____ , 20 _____

To: _____

RE: Credit Reference for _____ ,
      Account # _____ .

The above-named company has filed a credit application with our company naming your bank as a credit reference. By that application, the credit applicant has authorized us to contact the stated references and receive confidential information from them regarding their credit history. Attached please find a copy of the credit application naming your bank as a reference and authorizing our company to receive credit information.

We would, therefore, appreciate it if you could provide us with the following information:

1. How long has the company had an account with your bank?
2. What has been the average daily account balance?
3. Is there a history of overdrafts on this account?
4. Does this company currently have any loans with your bank?

   (a)   If so, what is the outstanding balance?
   (b)   Are they secured loans?
   (c)   What is the collateral?
   (d)   Has the repayment been satisfactory?

5. Has this customer been a satisfactory banking client?

We would appreciate any further information that you might be able to provide that may enable us to evaluate the credit history of this applicant. All information will be held in strict confidence. Thank you very much for your assistance.

_____
Signature

_____
Printed Name

Request for Trade Credit Reference

Date: _____ , 20 _____

To: _____

RE: Credit Reference for _____ ,
         Account # _____ .

The above-named company has filed a credit application with our company naming your company as a credit reference. By that application, the credit applicant has authorized us to contact the stated references and receive confidential information from them regarding their credit history. Attached please find a copy of the credit application naming your company as a reference and authorizing our company to receive credit information.

We would, therefore, appreciate it if you could provide us with the following information:

1. How long has the company had an account with your company?
2. What has been the average credit line of this company?
3. Is there a history of past due payments by this company?
4. What is the current credit balance owed you by this company?
5. Has the repayment been satisfactory?
6. What are the credit terms that you have extended to this customer?
7. Has this customer been a satisfactory customer?

We would appreciate any further information that you might be able to provide that may enable us to evaluate the credit history of this applicant. All information will be held in strict confidence. Thank you very much for your assistance.

_____
Signature

_____
Printed Name

Request for Credit Information

Date: _____ , 20 _____

To: _____

RE: Disclosure of Credit Information

By this letter, I hereby request complete disclosure of my personal credit file as held within your agency records. This request is in accordance with the Federal Fair Credit Reporting Act. I request that this disclosure provide the names and addresses of any parties who have received a copy of my credit report, and the names and addresses of any parties who have provided information that is contained in my credit report.

Name _____
Prior or other name _____
Address:

Prior or other address:

Social Security # _____   Phone _____

Dated: _____ , 20 _____

_____   _____
Signature   Printed Name

CHAPTER 14

Business Financing Documents

The documents included in this chapter are designed for use in situations in which businesspersons will be using personal property as collateral for a loan. Loans for real estate, other than a simple promissory note and mortgage or deed of trust, are generally subject to more state regulations and, thus, should be handled by a real estate professional or attorney.

The legal documents for financing of business loans generally employ three key documents, each of which serves a different purpose. First, there is the actual Promissory Note by which the borrower promises to repay a debt. These documents are covered in Chapter 15. Next is the Security Agreement by which the borrower puts up specific property as collateral for repayment of a loan. Finally, there is the U.C.C. Financing Statement that is used to record a lien against personal property in the public records.

All states have adopted a version of the Uniform Commercial Code (U.C.C.). This code is a set of detailed regulations which govern the purchase and sale of goods and financing arrangements, along with many other commercial transactions. Every state has a method of filing (on the public record) various statements relating to financing arrangements. The value of making timely filings of financing statements and other U.C.C. related matter is that the date and time of filing the statement *perfects* (or legally locks in the time) the security interest that has been bargained for. The party with the earliest perfected security interest relating to a particular piece of property has priority claim to that property.

Instructions

The various forms included in this chapter are as follows:

Security Agreement: This document is the document that provides the *secured party* (the party providing a loan) with the right to the collateral that the borrower has put up as security for the repayment of the loan.

The security agreement in this book provides for the following terms:

- That the borrower is granting the secured party a security interest in the property named

- That the security interest is to secure payment of a certain obligation
- That if the borrower defaults on the obligation, the secured party may accelerate the loan and make it immediately due and payable
- That if the borrower defaults, the secured party will have all the remedies under the U.C.C. (these may include selling the property or keeping the property)
- That the borrower will pay any costs of collection upon default
- That the borrower will be careful with the collateral and will not sell or dispose of it
- That the borrower will insure the collateral and keep it at a specified address for the term of the loan period
- That the borrower states that the property is owned free and clear, with no other liens against it, and that he or she has authority to use it as collateral
- That the borrower will sign any necessary financing statements
- That any changes to the agreement must be in writing

Receipt for Collateral: If it is desired that the property offered as collateral be held by the secured party, it will be necessary to alter the above Security Agreement by deleting Paragraphs 5 and 6 and preparing this receipt for the collateral. This receipt provides:

- That the secured party has obtained the collateral and will hold it as security until the loan is repaid
- That if the borrower defaults on the obligation, the property may be disposed of to satisfy the obligation
- That the borrower will pay any costs and expenses relating to holding the property
- That the secured party does not acknowledge the value or condition of the property offered as collateral

General Guaranty: This form provides for a guarantor for the repayment of a debt. This *guarantor* is, in effect, a co-signer for the obligation. The guarantor agrees that he or she will make the payments if any of the payments are late or not paid. The guarantor also agrees to pay any costs of collection if the guaranty is not lived up to. The guarantor also agrees that the guaranty may be enforced without having to first sue the borrower for defaulting on the debt. A mere default by the borrower without any court action will suffice to require the guarantor to make good on the obligation.

To fill in this form, use the names and addresses of the guarantor and secured party/noteholder and the number of days a payment by the guarantor may be late before it is considered a default on the guaranty.

Release of Security Interest: This form acts as a release of property from its nature as collateral for a loan. In addition, when the loan is repaid, the note or obligation should also be released (See Chapter 15). To fill in this form, simply provide the names and addresses of the parties and a description of the security interest being released.

U.C.C. Financing Statement: This form is a memorandum of the details of a security arrangement. It is designed to be filed with the appropriate state filing office in order to record the security interest. Once filed, this statement serves as a public record of the date and time that the security interest in the particular property was perfected. To fill in this form, simply provide the names and addresses of the parties and a description of the security interest being filed. The filing office will complete the form and stamp it or place a seal on it.

Release of U.C.C. Financing Statement: This form is a memorandum detailing the release of a financing obligation and should be filed with the state filing office to clear the records once the obligation has been satisfied. To fill in this form, simply provide the names and addresses of the parties and a description of the financing statement being released. The form will be completed by the filing office and stamped or sealed.

Security Agreement

This agreement is made on _____ , 20 _____ , between
_____ , borrower,
address:

and _____ , secured party,
address:

For valuable consideration, the parties agree as follows:

1. The borrower grants the secured party a security interest under Article 9 of the Uniform Commercial Code (U.C.C.) in the following personal property which will be considered collateral:

2. This security interest is granted to secure payment by the borrower to the secured party on the following obligation:

3. In the event of default by the borrower in payment of any of the amounts due on the obligation listed under Paragraph 2, the secured party may declare the entire obligation immediately due and payable and will have all of the remedies of a secured party under the Uniform Commercial Code.

4. In the event of such default, borrower will also be responsible for any costs of collection, including court costs and attorney fees.

5. The borrower agrees to use reasonable care in using the collateral and agrees not to sell or dispose of the collateral.

6. The borrower agrees to keep the collateral adequately insured and at the following address for the entire term of this security agreement:

7. The borrower represents that the collateral is owned free and clear and that there are no other security agreements, indebtedness, or liens relating to the property offered as collateral. Borrower also states that it has full authority to grant this security interest.

8. Borrower agrees to sign any financing statements that are required by the secured party to perfect this security interest.

9. No modification of this agreement will be effective unless it is in writing and is signed by both parties. This agreement binds and benefits both parties and any successors.

10. Time is of the essence of this agreement. This document, including any attachments, is the entire agreement between the parties. This agreement is governed by the laws of the State of _____ .

The parties have signed this agreement on the date specified at the beginning of this agreement.

_____
Signature of Borrower

_____
Printed Name of Borrower

_____
Signature of Secured Party

_____
Printed Name of Secured Party

Receipt for Collateral

This receipt is made in connection with the promissory note dated
_____ , 20 _____ , and the security agreement dated
_____ , 20 _____ , between
_____ , borrower,
address:

and _____ , noteholder/secured party,
address:

The noteholder/secured party acknowledges delivery of the following described personal property as collateral under the security agreement:

This collateral is subject to the lien and all of the conditions of the security agreement. In the event of the borrower's default on any of the terms of the note or security agreement, this property may be disposed of by the noteholder/secured party to satisfy any of the borrower's obligations as allowed by law.

The borrower will continue to pay all costs and expenses relating to this property, including any maintenance, storage fees, insurance, or taxes.

This receipt does not acknowledge the condition or the value of the property retained as collateral.

Dated: _____ , 20 _____

_____   _____
Signature of Borrower   Printed Name of Borrower

_____   _____
Signature of Noteholder/Secured Party   Printed Name of Noteholder/Secured Party

General Guaranty

This guaranty is made in connection with the promissory note dated _____ , 20 _____ , and the security agreement dated _____ , 20 _____ , between _____ , guarantor, of _____ ,

City of _____ , State of _____ , and _____ , secured party/noteholder, _____ ,

City of _____ , State of _____ .

For value received, the guarantor unconditionally guarantees payment of all payments on the above promissory note when due and satisfaction of all terms of the security agreement.

The guarantor waives demand, presentment for payment, protest, and notice, and agrees that the secured party/noteholder does not have to exhaust all rights against the borrower before demanding payment under this guaranty.

In the event that all payments due under this guaranty are not paid on demand within _____ days of demand, guarantor will also be responsible for any costs of collection on this note, including court costs and attorney fees.

This guaranty both binds and benefits both parties and any successors.

Dated: _____ , 20 _____

_____   _____
Signature of Guarantor   Signature of Secured Party/Noteholder

_____   _____
Printed Name of Guarantor   Printed Name of Secured Party/Noteholder

Release of Security Interest

For valuable consideration,

_____ , secured party,
address:

releases _____ , borrower,
address:

from the following specific security agreement, dated: _____ , 20 _____ :

Any claims or obligations that not specifically mentioned are not released by this release of security interest.

The secured party has not assigned any claims or obligations covered by this release to any other party.

The secured party will sign a release of U.C.C. financing statement if requested by borrower.

The party signing this release intends that it both bind and benefit any successors.

Dated: _____ , 20 _____

_____   _____
Signature of Secured Party   Printed Name of Secured Party

_____   _____
Signature of Borrower   Printed Name of Borrower

182

U.C.C. Financing Statement

This original Financing Statement is presented for filing under the U.C.C. (Uniform Commercial Code, as adopted in the following State of _____ .

(This Section for Use of the Filing Officer)

Date of filing _____   Time of filing _____
Number and address of filing office _____

_____

_____

Name(s) of Borrower _____
Address(es) of Borrower

Name(s) of Secured Party _____
Address(es) of Secured Party

This financing statement covers the following personal property:

This financing statement secures a debt document described as:

Name of document _____
Date of document _____ , 20 _____
Face value of document $ _____
Maturity date _____ , 20 _____

Related terms and conditions of the debt are contained in this debt document and any other documents mentioned in the debt document.

Dated: _____ , 20 _____   Seal

_____   _____
Signature of Borrower   Printed Name of Borrower

Release of U.C.C. Financing Statement

This Release of Financing Statement is presented for filing under the U.C.C. (Uniform Commercial Code, as adopted in the following State of _____ .

(This Section for Use of the Filing Officer)

Date of filing _____   Time of filing _____
Number and address of filing office _____

_____
_____

Name(s) of Borrower _____
Address(es) of Borrower

Name(s) of Secured Party _____
Address(es) of Secured Party

The original financing statement covers the following personal property:

File # of Original Financing Statement

Dated: _____ , 20 _____

Number and address where Original Financing Statement was filed

Dated: _____ , 20 _____   Seal

_____   _____
Signature of Secured Party   Printed Name of Secured Party

State of _____

County of _____

On _____ , 20 _____ , _____ personally
came before me and, being duly sworn, did state that he or she is the person described in the
above document and that he or she signed the above document in my presence.

_____
Signature of Notary Public

Notary Public, In and for the County of _____

State of _____

My commission expires: _____   Notary Seal

CHAPTER 15
Promissory Notes

Contained in this chapter are various promissory notes. A *promissory note* is a document by which a borrower promises to pay the holder of the note a certain amount of money under specific terms. In the forms in this chapter, the person who borrows the money is referred to as the *borrower* and the person whom the borrower is to pay is referred to as the *noteholder*. The noteholder is generally also the lender, but this need not be so. The forms in this chapter are intended for use only by businesses that are not regularly in the business of lending money. Complex state and federal regulations apply to lending institutions and such rules are beyond the scope of this book. Various forms for demanding payments on a promissory note are also included in this chapter.

Instructions

Promissory Note (Installment Repayment): This type of promissory note is a standard unsecured note. Being *unsecured* means that the *noteholder* (lender) has no collateral or specific property to foreclose against should the borrower default on the note. If the borrower doesn't pay, the noteholder must sue and get a general judgment against the borrower. Collection of the judgment may then be made against the borrower's assets.

This particular note calls for the borrower to pay a certain annual interest rate on the note and to make periodic payments to the noteholder. It also has certain general terms:

- That the borrower may prepay any amount on the note without penalty
- That if the borrower is in default, the noteholder may demand full payment on the note
- That the note is not assumable by anyone other than the borrower
- That the borrower waives certain formalities relating to demands for payment
- That the borrower agrees to pay any of the costs of collection after a default

In order to complete this form, the following information is necessary:

- The names and addresses of the borrower and the noteholder
- The amount of the principal of the loan
- The annual interest rate to be charged
- The period for the installments (for example, monthly or weekly)

- The amount due and the day of the period on which payments will be due
- The number of days a payment can be late before it is considered a default

Promissory Note (Lump Sum Repayment): This note is also an unsecured promise to pay. However, this version of a promissory note calls for the payment, including accrued interest, to be paid in one lump sum at a certain date in the future. This note has the same general conditions relating to prepayment, defaults, and assumability as the Promissory Note (Installment Repayment) discussed previously.

To prepare this form, use the following information:

- The names and addresses of the borrower and the noteholder
- The amount of the principal of the loan
- The annual interest rate to be charged
- The final due date of the lump-sum payment
- The number of days past the due date that the payment can be made before the note is in default

Promissory Note (on Demand): This also is an unsecured note. This type of promissory note, however, is immediately payable in full at any time upon the demand of the noteholder. This note has the same general conditions relating to prepayment, defaults, and assumability as the Promissory Note (Installment Repayment).

The following information is necessary to complete this form:

- The names and addresses of the borrower and the noteholder
- The amount of the principal of the loan
- The annual interest rate to be charged
- The number of days past the demand date that the payment can be made before the note is in default

Promissory Note (Secured): This type of promissory note is referred to as a *secured* note. What this means is that the borrower has given the noteholder some form of property or right to property as collateral for the loan. This allows the noteholder a direct claim against the specific property and the ability to foreclose against the property if the note is in default. A secured note also places the noteholder higher on the list for repayment if the borrower files for bankruptcy.

This particular form is designed to be used in conjunction with a completed Security Agreement (Chapter 14) covering the security arrangement between the borrower and the noteholder. The security for this type of note must be personal property. A secured promissory note may be drawn up for use with real estate as collateral. However, since this will entail the use of a mortgage or deed of trust as the Security Agreement, the services of a lawyer or real estate professional may be required. This secured promissory note is set up for installment payments. However, the language from a "demand" or "lump-sum" payment-type note can be substituted, if desired.

The conditions of this promissory note are as follows:

- That default on any of the conditions of the underlying security agreement may allow the noteholder to demand immediate full payment on the note
- That the borrower may prepay any amount on the note without penalty
- That if the borrower is in default, the noteholder may demand full payment on the note
- That the note is not assumable by anyone other than the borrower
- That the borrower waives certain formalities relating to demands for payment
- That the borrower agrees to pay any of the costs of collection after a default

The following information is needed to complete this form:

- The names and addresses of the borrower and the noteholder
- The amount of the principal of the loan
- The annual interest rate to be charged
- The period for the installments (for example, monthly or weekly)
- The amount due and the day of the period on which payments will be due
- The date of the security agreement which coincides with the note
- The number of days a payment can be late before it is considered a default

Promissory Note (with Guarantor): This type of note is also an unsecured one, but with an important difference. There is a guarantor for repayment of the debt. This *guarantor* is, in effect, a co-signer for the note. The guarantor agrees that if any of the payments are late or not paid, they will make the payments. The guarantor also agrees to pay any costs of collection if the guaranty is not lived up to. This unsecured promissory note is set up for installment payments. However, the language from a "demand" or "lump-sum" payment-type note can be used instead, if desired.

To fill in this form, use the following information:

- The names and addresses of the borrower and the noteholder
- The amount of the principal of the loan
- The annual interest rate to be charged
- The period for the installments (for example, monthly or weekly)
- The amount due and the day of the period on which payments will be due
- The number of days a payment by the borrower can be late before it is considered a default by the borrower

- The name and address of the guarantor
- The number of days a payment by the guarantor can be late before it is considered a default by the guarantor

Release of Promissory Note: This release is intended to be used to release a party from obligations under a Promissory Note. There are several other methods by which to accomplish this same objective. The return of the original note to the maker, clearly marked "Paid In Full," will serve the same purpose. A Receipt in Full will also accomplish this goal. The Release of Promissory Note may, however, be used in those situations when the release is based on something other than payment in full of the underlying note. For example, the note may be satisfied by a gift from the bearer of the note of release from the obligation. Another situation may involve a release of the note based on a concurrent release of a claim which the maker of the note holds against the holder of the note.

Demand and Notice of Default on Installment Promissory Note: This form will be used to notify the *maker* (the borrower) of a promissory note of his or her default on an installment payment on a promissory note. Notice of default should be sent promptly to any account which falls behind in its payments on a note. This notice provides a legal basis for a suit for breach of the promissory note.

Demand and Notice for Full Payment on Installment Promissory Note: A demand for full payment on a promissory note can only be made if the precise terms of the note allow for this. A note may have specific terms which allow it to be accelerated upon default on any payments. This means that if the maker of the note falls behind on his or her payments, the holder may accelerate all of the payment dates to the present and demand that the note be paid in full. Generally, this form will be used after giving the debtor a reasonable time to make up the missed installment payment.

Demand and Notice for Payment on Demand Promissory Note: This document should be used when you hold a promissory note which is payable on demand and you wish to demand full payment. Realistically, you should generally allow the maker of such a note a reasonable amount of time to gather enough funds to make the payment. This form allows a period of 10 days. However, you may wish to modify this period after consulting with the debtor.

Demand and Notice for Payment from Guarantor on Demand Promissory Note: This form is intended for use if the defaulted-upon note has been guaranteed by a third party. Any such guaranty should, generally, be clearly noted on the face of the note. This demand notifies the guarantor of the default of the maker of the note and demands that the guarantor live up to the promise to pay upon the default of the maker.

Promissory Note (Installment Repayment)

$ _____

Dated: _____ , 20 _____

For value received,

_____ , borrower,
address:

promises to pay

_____ , noteholder,
address:

the principal amount of $ _____ , with interest at the annual rate of
_____ percent, on any unpaid balance.

Payments are payable to the noteholder in _____ consecutive installments of
$ _____ , including interest, and continuing on the _____ day
of each _____ until paid in full. If not paid off sooner, this note is due and payable
in full on _____ , 20 _____ .

This note may be prepaid in whole or in part at any time without penalty. If the borrower
is in default more than _____ days with any payment, this note is payable
upon demand of any noteholder. This note is not assumable without the written consent of
the noteholder. The borrower waives demand, presentment for payment, protest, and notice.
In the event of any default, borrower will be responsible for any costs of collection on this
note, including court costs and attorney fees.

_____
Signature of Borrower

_____
Printed Name of Borrower

Promissory Note (Lump Sum Repayment)

$ _____

Dated: _____ , 20 _____

For value received,

_____ , borrower,

address:

promises to pay

_____ , noteholder,

address:

the principal amount of $ _____ , with interest at the annual rate of _____ percent, on any unpaid balance.

Payment on this note is due and payable to the noteholder in full on or before _____ , 20 _____ .

This note may be prepaid in whole or in part at any time without penalty. If the borrower is in default more than _____ days with any payment, this note is payable upon demand of any noteholder. This note is not assumable without the written consent of the noteholder. The borrower waives demand, presentment for payment, protest, and notice. In the event of any default, the borrower will be responsible for any costs of collection on this note, including court costs and attorney fees.

_____

Signature of Borrower

_____

Printed Name of Borrower

Promissory Note (on Demand)

$ _____

Dated: _____ , 20 _____

For value received,

_____ , borrower,

address:

promises to pay ON DEMAND to

_____ , noteholder,

address:

the principal amount of $ _____ , with interest at the annual rate of
_____ percent, on any unpaid balance.

This note may be prepaid in whole or in part at any time without penalty. This note is not assumable without the written consent of the noteholder. The borrower waives demand, presentment for payment, protest, and notice. In the event of such default of over _____ days in making payment, the borrower will be also be responsible for any costs of collection on this note, including court costs and attorney fees.

_____
Signature of Borrower

_____
Printed Name of Borrower

Promissory Note (Secured)

$ _____

Dated: _____ , 20 _____

For value received,

_____ , borrower,

address:

promises to pay

_____ , noteholder,

address:

the principal amount of $ _____ , with interest at the annual rate of _____ percent, on any unpaid balance.

Payments are payable to the noteholder in _____ consecutive installments of $ _____ , including interest, and continuing on the _____ day of each _____ until paid in full. If not paid off sooner, this note is due and payable in full on _____ , 20 _____ .

This note is secured by a security agreement dated _____ , 20 _____ , which has also been signed by the borrower. This note may be accelerated and demand for immediate full payment made by the noteholder upon breach of any conditions of the security agreement. This note may be prepaid in whole or in part at any time without penalty. If the borrower is in default more than _____ days with any payment, this note is payable upon demand of any noteholder. This note is not assumable without the written consent of the noteholder. The borrower waives demand, presentment for payment, protest, and notice. In the event of any default, the borrower will be responsible for any costs of collection on this note, including court costs and attorney fees.

_____
Signature of Borrower

_____
Printed Name of Borrower

Promissory Note (with Guarantor)

$ _____

Dated: _____ , 20 _____

For value received,

_____ , borrower,

address:

promises to pay

_____ , noteholder,

address:

the principal amount of $ _____ , with interest at the annual rate of _____ % (_____ percent), on any unpaid balance.

Payments are payable to the noteholder in _____ consecutive installments of $ _____ , including interest, and continuing on the _____ day of each _____ until paid in full. If not paid off sooner, this note is due and payable in full on _____ , 20 _____ .

This note may be prepaid in whole or in part at any time without penalty. If the borrower is in default more than _____ days with any payment, this note is payable upon demand of any noteholder. This note is not assumable without the written consent of the noteholder. The borrower waives demand, presentment for payment, protest, and notice. In the event of any default, the borrower will be responsible for any costs of collection on this note, including court costs and attorney fees.

_____

Signature of Borrower

_____

Printed Name of Borrower

Guaranty

For value received,

_____ , guarantor,

address:

unconditionally guarantees payment of all payments on the above promissory note when due.

The guarantor waives demand, presentment for payment, protest, and notice, and agrees that the noteholder does not have to exhaust all rights against the borrower before demanding payment under this guaranty.

In the event that all payments due under this guaranty are not paid on demand within _____ days of demand, guarantor will be responsible for any costs of collection on this note, including court costs and attorney fees.

This guaranty both binds and benefits both parties and any successors.

Dated: _____ , 20 _____

_____

Signature of Guarantor

_____

Printed Name of Guarantor

Release of Promissory Note

In consideration of full payment of the promissory note dated
_____ , 20 _____ , in the face amount of $ _____ ,
_____ , noteholder,
address:

releases and discharges
_____ , borrower(s),
address:

from any claims or obligations on account of this note.

The party signing this release intends that it bind and benefit both itself and any successors.

Dated: _____ , 20 _____

_____
Signature of Noteholder

_____
Printed Name of Noteholder

Demand and Notice of Default on Installment Promissory Note

Date: _____ , 20 _____

To: _____

RE: Default on Installment Promissory Note

Dear _____ :

Regarding the promissory note dated _____ , 20 _____ , in the original amount of $ _____ , of which you are the maker, you have defaulted on the installment payment due on _____ , 20 _____ , in the amount of $ _____ .

Demand is made upon you for payment of this past-due installment payment. If payment is not received by us within ten (10) days from the date of this notice, we will proceed to enforce our rights under the promissory note for collection of the entire balance.

Very truly,

_____
Signature of Noteholder

_____
Printed Name of Noteholder

Demand and Notice for Full Payment on Installment Promissory Note

Date: _____ , 20 _____

To: _____

RE: Full Payment on Installment Promissory Note

Dear _____ :

I am currently the holder of your promissory note dated _____ , 20 _____ , in the amount of $ _____ , which is payable to _____ , noteholder address and phone number:

You have been given previous notice on _____ , 20 _____ , of your default on payments of this note. Under the terms of the note and by this notice, I am making a formal demand for payment by you of the full unpaid balance of this note, together with all accrued interest within ten (10) days of receipt of this letter. Please contact me at the above address and phone number in order to initiate the payment process. If full payment is not received within ten (10) days from the date of this demand, the note shall be forwarded to our attorneys for legal collection proceedings and you will be immediately liable for all costs of collection, including additional legal and court costs. Thank you very much for your prompt attention to this serious matter.

Very truly,

_____
Signature of Noteholder

_____
Printed Name of Noteholder

Demand and Notice for Payment on Demand Promissory Note

Date: _____ , 20 _____

To: _____

RE: Payment on Demand Promissory Note

Dear _____ :

I am currently the holder of your promissory note dated _____ , 20 _____ , in the amount of $ _____ , which is payable to
_____ , the original noteholder, or
to _____ , the holder on demand.

By this notice, I am making a formal demand for payment by you of the full unpaid balance of this note, together with all accrued interest, within ten (10) days of receipt of this letter. The total amount due at this time is $ _____ .

Please contact me at the address and phone number below in order to initiate the payment process. If full payment is not received within ten (10) days from the date of this demand, the note shall be forwarded to our attorneys for legal collection proceedings and you will be immediately liable for all costs of collection, including any additional legal and court costs. Thank you very much for your prompt attention to this serious matter.

Very truly,

_____
Signature of Current Noteholder

_____
Printed Name of Current Noteholder

_____
Address of Current Noteholder

_____
Phone Number of Current Noteholder

Demand and Notice for Payment from Guarantor on Demand Promissory Note

Date: _____ , 20 _____

To: _____

RE: Payment from Guarantor on Demand Promissory Note

Dear _____ :

I am currently the holder of a promissory note dated _____ , 20 _____ , in the amount of $ _____ , where the maker is _____ , and you are the guarantor. This note is payable to _____ , the holder on demand.

Please be advised that on _____ , 20 _____ , notice and demand for payment was made to the maker of the note and payment has not been forthcoming. By this notice, I am making a formal demand for immediate payment by you, the guarantor, of the full unpaid balance of this note, together with all interest.

Please contact me at the following address:

and phone number _____ , in order to initiate the payment process.

If full payment is not received within ten (10) days from the date of this demand, the note shall be forwarded to our attorneys for legal collection proceedings and you will be immediately liable for all costs of collection, including any additional legal and court costs. Thank you very much for your prompt attention to this serious matter.

Very truly,

_____
Signature of Current Noteholder

_____
Printed Name of Current Noteholder

CHAPTER 16

Purchase of Goods Documents

The documents in this chapter are all related to the purchase and sale of goods from the perspective of the business doing the purchasing. The purchase and sale of goods in business situations is governed by the Uniform Commercial Code (U.C.C.) as it has been adopted by the various states. The forms in this chapter are intended to be used to comply with the provisions of the U.C.C. and protect your rights.

Instructions

Request for Price Quote: This form is used to obtain a firm price quote for particular goods. It allows the purchaser to lock in the price for a certain time period and bars the seller from raising the price during that period.

Notice of Acceptance of Order: This form provides for acceptance of an order and acknowledgment that the order has been inspected and approved by the purchaser.

Notice of Conditional Acceptance of Non-Conforming Goods: When a purchaser receives a shipment of goods that does not conform to the order that was placed, the purchaser may offer to accept the goods on the condition that the purchase price be adjusted to accommodate for the non-conformity of the goods. The seller, of course, has the right to reject any discount and request that the goods be returned. This form allows for a conditional acceptance of the goods and requests that a price reduction be allowed within 10 days.

Notice of Rejection of Non-Conforming Goods: Use this form after the above form has been used and the 10-day period for acceptance of the price reduction terms has expired. This forms notifies the seller that the goods have been fully rejected for non-conformity with the original purchase order. It also gives the seller 10 days to return the money paid for the goods and 10 days to arrange for return of the goods. If the money is not returned, the advice of an attorney versed in business law should be sought.

Notice of Conditional Acceptance of Defective Goods: When a purchaser receives a shipment of goods that is defective or damaged in some manner, the purchaser may offer to accept the goods on the condition that the purchase price be adjusted to accommodate for the defect in the goods. The seller, of course, has the right to reject any discount and request that the goods be returned. This form allows for a conditional acceptance of the goods and requests that a price reduction be allowed within 10 days.

Notice of Rejection of Defective Goods: This form should be used after using the above form and after the 10-day period for acceptance of the price reduction terms has expired. This form notifies the seller that the goods have been fully rejected because of defects. It also gives the seller 10 days to return the money paid for the goods and 10 days to arrange for return of the goods. If the money is not returned, the advice of an attorney versed in business law should be sought.

Notice of Rejection of Order: This form is a generic form for the rejection of an order by the purchaser. In addition to rejection of an order for non-conformity or for defective goods, orders may be rejected for unreasonable delay in shipment, damage, partial shipment only, that the price charged was not what was quoted, etc. It gives the seller 10 days to return the money paid for the goods. If the money is not returned, the advice of a business attorney should be sought.

Notice of Refusal to Accept Delivery: This form should be used in those situations when the actual delivery of the goods is rejected (for example, when physical damage is evident on immediate inspection).

Notice of Demand for Delivery of Goods: The use of this form is required in situations in which goods have been ordered and paid for, but not delivered. This notifies the seller of a demand for immediate shipment of the goods or return of the money.

Notice of Cancellation of Purchase Order: After the use of the previous form notifying the seller of a demand for delivery of goods and after the expiration of the 10-day period set for delivery by the above notice, this form should be sent to the seller. It effectively cancels the original purchase order for non-delivery and demands the return of any money paid. If the money is not returned, the advice of an attorney competent in business law should be sought.

Notice of Return of Goods Sold on Approval: When a purchaser receives goods *on approval*, he or she is allowed to examine the goods for a certain period and return them to the seller if desired within that time frame. This form is used to notify the seller of the decision to return the goods sold on approval.

Request for Price Quote

Date: _____ , 20 _____

To: _____

RE: Request for Price Quote

Dear _____ :

We are interested in purchasing the following goods:

Please provide us with a firm quote for your standard price for these goods and the time period during which this quote will be good. Also, please provide us with your discount schedule for volume purchases. Please also provide us with the following information regarding any order that we might place with your company:

1. The standard terms for payment of invoices
2. The availability of an open credit account with your firm. (If available, please provide us with the appropriate credit application)
3. Any delivery costs for orders. (If these costs are included in the price quote, please indicate on the quote)
4. Any sales or other taxes. (If these costs are included in the price quote, please indicate)
5. The usual delivery time for orders from the date of your receipt of a purchase order to our receipt of the goods

Very truly,

_____
Signature

_____
Printed Name

Notice of Acceptance of Order

Date: _____ , 20 _____

To: _____

RE: Acceptance of Order

Dear _____ :

Please be advised that we have received the following goods, pursuant to our purchase order # _____ , dated _____ , 20 _____ :

The goods are further identified by invoice # _____ and bill of lading/ packing slip # _____ .

Please be advised that we have inspected the goods and they have been received in good condition, with no defects, and in conformity with our order.

Accordingly, we accept this shipment of goods.

Very truly,

_____
Signature

_____
Printed Name

Notice of Conditional Acceptance
of Non-Conforming Goods

Date: _____ , 20 _____

To: _____

RE: Conditional Acceptance of Non-Conforming Goods

Dear _____ :

On _____ , 20 _____ , we received delivery from you on our purchase order # _____ , dated _____ , 20 _____ . The goods which were delivered at that time do not conform to the specifications that were provided with our purchase order for the following reasons:

Although these goods are non-conforming and we are not obligated to accept them, we are prepared to accept these goods on the condition that you credit our account with you for $ _____ . This credit will make the total price of the goods under this purchase order $ _____ .

If you do not accept this proposal within ten (10) days from the date of this notice, we will reject these goods as non-conforming and they will be returned to you.

Please be advised that we reserve all of our rights under the Uniform Commercial Code and any other applicable laws.

Thank you for your immediate attention to this matter.

Very truly,

_____   _____
Signature   Printed Name

Notice of Rejection of Non-Conforming Goods

Date: _____ , 20 _____

To: _____

RE: Rejection of Non-Conforming Goods

Dear _____ :

On _____ , 20 _____ , we received delivery from you on our purchase order # _____ , dated _____ , 20 _____ . The goods which were delivered at that time do not conform to the specifications that were provided with our purchase order for the following reasons:

We paid for these goods by our check # _____ , dated _____ , 20 _____ , in the amount of $ _____ . This check has been cashed by you.

By this notice, we reject the delivery of these goods and demand the return of our money. Unless we receive a refund of our money within ten (10) days of the date of this letter, we will take immediate legal action for the return of our money. Please further advise us as to your wishes for the return of the rejected goods at your expense. Unless we receive return instructions within ten (10) days of this letter, we accept no responsibility for the safe storage of these goods.

Please be advised that we reserve all of our rights under the Uniform Commercial Code and any other applicable laws.

Thank you for your immediate attention to this matter.

Very truly,

_____   _____
Signature   Printed Name

Notice of Conditional Acceptance
of Defective Goods

Date: _____ , 20 _____

To: _____

RE: Conditional Acceptance of Defective Goods

Dear _____ :

On _____ , 20 _____ , we received delivery from you on our purchase order # _____ , dated _____ , 20 _____ . The goods which were delivered at that time were defective for the following reasons:

Although these goods are defective and we are not obligated to accept them, we are prepared to accept these goods on the condition that you credit our account with you for $ _____ . This credit will make the total price of the goods under this purchase order $ _____ .

If you do not accept this proposal within ten (10) days from the date of this notice, we will reject these goods as defective and they will be returned to you.

Please be advised that we reserve all of our rights under the Uniform Commercial Code and any other applicable laws.

Thank you for your immediate attention to this matter.

Very truly,

_____   _____
Signature   Printed Name

Notice of Rejection of Defective Goods

Date: _____ , 20 _____

To: _____

RE: Rejection of Defective Goods

Dear _____ :

On _____ , 20 _____ , we received delivery from you on our purchase order # _____ , dated _____ , 20 _____ . The goods which were delivered at that time were defective for the following reasons:

We paid for these goods by our check # _____ , dated _____ , 20 _____ , in the amount of $ _____ . This check has been cashed by you.

By this notice, we reject the delivery of these goods and demand the return of our money. Unless we receive a refund of our money within ten (10) days of the date of this letter, we will take immediate legal action for the return of our money. Please further advise us as to your wishes for the return of the rejected goods at your expense. Unless we receive instructions for their return within ten (10) days of this letter, we accept no responsibility for the safe storage of these goods.

Please be advised that we reserve all of our rights under the Uniform Commercial Code and any other applicable laws.

Thank you for your immediate attention to this matter.

Very truly,

_____   _____
Signature   Printed Name

Notice of Rejection of Order

Date: _____ , 20 _____

To: _____

RE: Rejection of Order

Dear _____ :

On _____ , 20 _____ , we received delivery from you on our purchase order # _____ , dated _____ , 20 _____ . We reject these goods for the following reasons:

We paid for these goods by our check # _____ , dated _____ , 20 _____ , in the amount of $ _____ . This check has been cashed by you.

By this notice, we reject the delivery of these goods and demand the return of our money. Unless we receive a refund of our money within ten (10) days of the date of this letter, we will take immediate legal action for the return of our money. Please further advise us as to your wishes for the return of the rejected goods at your expense. Unless we receive instructions for their return within ten (10) days of this letter, we accept no responsibility for the safe storage of these goods.

Please be advised that we reserve all of our rights under the Uniform Commercial Code and any other applicable laws.

Thank you for your immediate attention to this matter.

Very truly,

_____   _____
Signature   Printed Name

Notice of Refusal to Accept Delivery

Date: _____ , 20 _____

To: _____

RE: Refusal to Accept Delivery

Dear _____ :

On _____ , 20 _____ , we received delivery from you on our purchase order # _____ , dated _____ , 20 _____ . We do not accept delivery of these goods for the following reasons:

We paid for these goods by our check # _____ , dated _____ , 20 _____ , in the amount of $ _____ . This check has been cashed by you.

By this notice, we refuse to accept the delivery of these goods and demand the return of our money. Unless we receive a refund of our money within ten (10) days of the date of this letter, we will take immediate legal action for the return of our money.

Please be advised that we reserve all of our rights under the Uniform Commercial Code and any other applicable laws.

Thank you for your immediate attention to this matter.

Very truly,

_____   _____
Signature   Printed Name

Notice of Demand for Delivery of Goods

Date: _____ , 20 _____

To: _____

RE: Demand for Delivery of Goods

Dear _____ :

On _____ , 20 _____ , by our purchase order
_____ , a copy of which is enclosed, we ordered the following goods
from you:

We paid for these goods by our check # _____ , dated _____ ,
20 _____ , in the amount of $ _____ . This check has been cashed by you.

To date, the goods have not been delivered to us. We, therefore, demand the immediate delivery of these goods. Unless the goods are delivered to us within ten (10) days of the date of this letter, we will take action to cancel this purchase order and have our money returned.

Please be advised that we reserve all of our rights under the Uniform Commercial Code and any other applicable laws.

Thank you for your immediate attention to this matter.

Very truly,

_____   _____
Signature   Printed Name

Notice of Cancellation of Purchase Order

Date: _____ , 20 _____

To: _____

RE: Cancellation of Purchase Order

Dear _____ :

On _____ , 20 _____ , by our purchase order
_____ , a copy of which is enclosed, we ordered the following goods
from you:

We paid for these goods by our check # _____ , dated _____ ,
20 _____ , in the amount of $ _____ . This check has been cashed by you.

On _____ , 20 _____ , we demanded immediate delivery of the goods.
To date, the goods have not been delivered to us.

By this notice, we, therefore, cancel this order for late delivery and demand the immediate return of our money. Unless we receive a refund of our money within ten (10) days of the date of this letter, we will take immediate legal action for the return of our money.

Please be advised that we reserve all of our rights under the Uniform Commercial Code and any other applicable laws.

Thank you for your immediate attention to this matter.

Very truly,

_____   _____
Signature   Printed Name

Notice of Return of Goods Sold on Approval

Date: _____ , 20 _____

To: _____

RE: Return of Goods Sold on Approval

Dear _____ :

On _____ , 20 _____ , by our purchase order
_____ , a copy of which is enclosed, we received the following goods
from you on approval:

Please be advised that at this time we are electing to return these goods to you.

Thank you very much for the opportunity to examine the goods.

Very truly,

_____   _____
Signature   Printed Name

CHAPTER 17
Sale of Goods Documents

The various forms included in this chapter are also intended to be used for situations involving the sale of goods. However, these forms are prepared for use by the seller.

The first set are forms to be used in response to a buyer's action after goods have been shipped. Two legal contracts relating to the sale of goods are also included. Finally, two documents relating to the bulk sales of business inventory are also included.

In addition to the forms in this chapter, throughout this book there are other forms that may be used by a business which sells products. For example, Bills of Sale (Chapter 10), collection of accounts (Chapter 18), Promissory Notes (Chapter 15), etc. may all be valuable at some time during the normal course of business.

Instructions

Demand for Explanation of Rejected Goods: Use of this form will follow a seller's notification that the buyer has rejected goods. It demands a satisfactory explanation for the rejection. To complete this form, specify the date, name of buyer, purchase order number, type of goods shipped, and date of rejection of the goods.

Notice of Replacement of Rejected Goods: This notice is to be used to replace goods that have been reasonably rejected by a buyer. It also instructs the buyer to return the rejected goods at the seller's expense. To complete this form, specify the date, name of buyer, purchase order number, type of goods shipped, and date of rejection of the goods.

Notice of Goods Sold on Approval: When goods are sold to a buyer on approval, this form should be used to specify the time period that the buyer has to examine the goods and either accept or return them.

Contract for Sale of Goods: This basic contract is for the one-time sale of specific goods. To properly complete this document, the following information is necessary:

- The names and addresses of the seller and buyer
- A description of the goods being sold
- Any specifications that the buyer wishes to place on the goods

- The cost of the goods and the terms of payment
- The delivery date required by the buyer
- The amount of shipping costs and which party is to pay for the shipping
- Any additional terms of the sale
- The state whose laws will govern the contract

Contract for Sale of Goods on Consignment: For the sale of goods to a buyer on *consignment* (for resale), this form should be used. It provides that the seller will deliver goods to the buyer and that the buyer will display and attempt to resell the goods. It also provides that the goods remain the property of the seller until sold and that the buyer must return any unsold goods on demand. The following information will be used to prepare this document:

- The names and addresses of the seller and buyer
- A description of the goods being sold
- The cost of the goods and the terms of payment
- The price set for the goods
- The delivery date required by the buyer
- The amount of shipping costs and which party is to pay for the shipping
- Any additional terms of the sale
- The state whose laws will govern the contract

Bulk Transfer Affidavit: The Uniform Commercial Code (U.C.C.) contains provisions that are designed to protect both potential buyers and creditors of businesses that intend to make bulk transfers of their inventory. Failure to comply with the Bulk Sales or Transfers Act portion of the U.C.C. will generally mean that original creditors of a seller will have a lien against the *assets* (inventory) which are transferred to the buyer. This form is to be used by a seller to inform the buyer of all creditors of the business and the amount of their claims against the business.

To complete, simply list the seller's state and county and the seller's and buyer's names and addresses, and attach a separate sheet detailing the names, addresses, and amount claimed by all known creditors and listing the state whose laws will govern the contract. If there are no creditors or if the Bulk Sales and Transfers Act does not apply to a particular sale, this form may also be used as an affidavit to such facts by noting "None" on the attached sheet.

Bulk Transfer Notice: This form is to be used to provide notice to the creditors of the intended bulk sale of goods. To complete, simply fill in the buyer's and seller's names and addresses, date of the sales agreement, proposed closing date of the sale, and the state in which the sale will take place. A copy of this completed form should be supplied to each creditor.

Demand for Explanation of Rejected Goods

Date: _____ , 20 _____

To: _____

RE: Explanation of Rejected Goods

Dear _____ :

On _____ , 20 _____ , we shipped the following goods to you pursuant to your purchase order # _____ , dated _____ , 20 _____ :

On _____ , 20 _____ , we received notice that you had rejected delivery of these goods without satisfactory explanation. We, therefore, request that you provide us with an adequate explanation for this rejection. Unless we are provided with such explanation within ten (10) days, we will take legal action to obtain payment for these goods.

Please be advised that we reserve all of our rights under the Uniform Commercial Code and any other applicable laws.

Thank you for your immediate attention to this matter.

Very truly,

_____   _____
Signature   Printed Name

Notice of Replacement of Rejected Goods

Date: _____ , 20 _____

To: _____

RE: Replacement of Rejected Goods

Dear _____ :

On _____ , 20 _____ , we shipped the following goods to you pursuant to your purchase order # _____ , dated _____ , 20 _____ :

On _____ , 20 _____ , we received notice that you had rejected delivery of these goods.

Please return the rejected goods to us at our expense using the same carrier that delivered the goods.

In addition, please be advised that we are shipping replacement goods to you at our expense.

If this correction of the rejected goods is not satisfactory, please contact us immediately. We apologize for any problems this may have caused.

Very truly,

_____   _____
Signature   Printed Name

Notice of Goods Sold on Approval

Date: _____ , 20 _____

To: _____

RE: Goods Sold on Approval

Dear _____ :

Please be advised that the following goods are being delivered to you on approval:

If these goods do not meet your requirements, you may return all or a part of them at our expense within _____ days of your receipt of the goods.

Any of these goods sold on approval that have not been returned to us by that time will be considered accepted by you and you will be charged accordingly.

We trust that you will find our goods satisfactory. Thank you very much for your business.

Very truly,

_____   _____
Signature   Printed Name

Contract for Sale of Goods

This contract for sale of goods is made on _____ , 20 _____ , between
_____ , seller, of
_____ ,
City of _____ , State of _____ , and
_____ , buyer, of
_____ ,
City of _____ , State of _____ .

For valuable consideration, the parties agree as follows:

1. The seller agrees to sell and the buyer agrees to buy the following goods:

2. The seller agrees to provide goods which meet the following specifications:

3. The buyer agrees to pay the following price(s) for the goods:

4. The seller agrees that the goods will be delivered to the buyer's place of business by _____ , 20 _____ . The shipping costs are estimated at $ _____ , and will be paid by the _____ .

5. The seller represents that it has legal title to the goods and full authority to sell the goods. Seller also represents that the property is sold free and clear of all liens, mortgages, indebtedness, or liabilities.

6. Any additional terms:

7. No modification of this contract will be effective unless it is in writing and is signed by both parties. Time is of the essence of this contract. This contract binds and benefits both the buyer and seller and any successors. This document, including any attachments, is the entire agreement between the buyer and seller. This contract is governed by the laws of the State of _____ .

The parties have signed this contract on the date specified at the beginning of this contract.

_____
Signature of Seller

_____
Signature of Buyer

_____
Printed Name of Seller

_____
Printed Name of Buyer

Contract for Sale of Goods on Consignment

This contract for sale of goods on consignment is made on
_____ , 20 _____ , between
_____ , seller, of

_____ ,
City of _____ , State of _____ , and
_____ , buyer, of

_____ ,
City of _____ , State of _____ .

For valuable consideration, the parties agree as follows:

1. The seller agrees to provide the following goods to the buyer on consignment:

2. The buyer agrees to display the goods at its place of business and use its best efforts to resell the goods at the following price(s):

3. The goods will remain the property of the seller until they are resold by the buyer. The buyer agrees to pay the following price(s) to the seller for any goods sold while held on consignment under this contract:

4. The seller agrees that the goods will be delivered to the buyer's place of business by
_____ , 20 _____ . The shipping costs are estimated at
$ _____ , and will be paid by the _____ .

5. The buyer agrees to return any unsold goods, in good condition, to the seller on the seller's written demand.

6. The seller represents that it has legal title to the goods and full authority to sell the goods. Seller also represents that the property is sold free and clear of all liens, mortgages, indebtedness, or liabilities.

7. Any additional terms:

8. No modification of this contract will be effective unless it is in writing and is signed by both parties. Time is of the essence of this contract. This contract binds and benefits both the buyer and seller and any successors. This document, including any attachments, is the entire agreement between the buyer and seller. This contract is governed by the laws of the State of _____ .

The parties have signed this contract on the date specified at the beginning of this contract.

_____
Signature of Seller

_____
Signature of Buyer

_____
Printed Name of Seller

_____
Printed Name of Buyer

Bulk Transfer Affidavit

State of _____

County of _____

I, _____ , of

_____ ,

City of _____ , State of _____ , being of legal age, make the following statements and declare that, on my own personal knowledge, they are true:

1. I am the seller of business assets of

    _____ , located at

    _____ ,

    City of _____ , State of _____ , under an agreement

    dated _____ , 20 _____ , with

    _____ , buyer, located at

    _____ ,

    City of _____ , State of _____ .

2. This affidavit is provided to the buyer, under provisions of the Uniform Commercial Code, as enacted in the State of _____ , for the purpose of providing creditors with notice of the intended sale under this agreement. Attached to and made part of this affidavit is a true and complete list of the names, addresses, and amounts due all creditors of the seller's business as of this date.

Signed under the penalty of perjury on _____ , 20 _____ .

_____

Signature of Seller

_____

Printed Name of Seller

Bulk Transfer Notice

Date: _____ , 20 _____

To: _____

RE: Notice to Creditors

Dear _____ :

Please take notice that
_____ , located at
_____ ,
City of _____ , State of _____ , under an agreement
dated _____ , 20 _____ , with
_____ , buyer, located at
_____ ,
City of _____ , State of _____ , intends to make a bulk sale
or transfer of business assets. The seller has not done business under any other name for the
past three (3) years. As part of this proposed sale, all debts of the seller are to be paid in full
as due. This sale is intended to take place on _____ , 20 _____ .

This notice is provided in compliance with the Bulk Sales or Transfers Act of the Uniform
Commercial Code, as enacted in the State of _____ .

As a creditor of the business being sold, you are notified to send verification of all bills, invoices, or records of accounts due to the buyer and seller at the above addresses.

_____
Signature of Seller

Signature of Buyer
_____

_____
Printed Name of Seller

Printed Name of Buyer
_____

CHAPTER 18
Collection Documents

The documents contained in this chapter are for use in the collection of past-due payments owed to you. Through the proper use of the documents in this chapter, your business should be able to collect on the majority of overdue and unpaid accounts without having to resort to the use of attorneys or collection agencies. Of course, if the initial attempts at collection using these documents fail, then it is advisable to turn the accounts over to parties who will be able to bring legal procedures to bear on the defaulting parties. The following forms are included in this chapter:

Instructions

Request for Payment: This form should be used to make the initial request for payment from an overdue account payable. It should be sent when you have decided that an account is in delinquent status. It is intended to promote payment on the overdue account. To prepare this form, you will need to enter the name of the company or person with the delinquent account; the date, amount, and invoice numbers of the past-due invoices; any interest or late charges which have been assessed; and any credits or payments which have been made on the account. Be sure to keep a record of this request. Generally, making a copy of the actual request that is sent and placing in the file for the overdue account is the easiest method for this.

Second Request for Payment: You will generally use this form on the next billing date after you have sent the first request for payment. The information necessary for this form will be the same as the first request. You will need, however, to update any additions or subtractions to the account which have taken place during the period since the first request (for example, any payments on account, additional interest charges, additional late payments, additional invoices, etc.).

Final Demand for Payment: This form should normally be used after one more billing cycle has elapsed since the second payment request was sent. It is a notice that collection proceedings will be begun if payment has not been received on the delinquent account within 10 days. (Please note that you may extend this period if you desire, for example, to allow for 30 days to pay). This notice should not be sent unless you actually plan on following up with the collection. However, it is often reasonable to wait a short while after the deadline before proceeding with assignment of the account for collection. This allows for delays in mail delivery and takes into account the tendency of companies and people with debt problems to push the time limits to the maximum.

Assignment of Account for Collection: This document is one of the methods to follow-up the final demand for payment. With this document, the past-due account is entirely turned over to either a collection agency or attorney for further collection procedures. This form is an actual assignment of the account to the firm who then actually owns the account and will continue any attempts at collection. It provides that the *assignee* (the firm who will be taking over the collection procedures) pays your company (the *assignor*, or the "one who assigns") an amount for the rights to collect the account. The fee paid is generally a percentage of the amount due. For example, if the fee is fifty percent and you are owed $4,000.00 on the account, the assignee firm will pay you $2,000.00 for taking over the account. Of course, if they are successful in collecting the entire amount they will have earned an additional $2,000.00. But at least you will have gotten half of the money owed to you. Under this method of collection, all future payments are to be paid to the assignee firm. Another method for handling collection is provided below in the Appointment of Collection Agent form.

Notice of Assignment of Account for Collection: This form is used to notify the customer that the past-due account has been formally assigned to the collection firm. It tells the customer to make future payments on the account to the collection firm.

Appointment of Collection Agent: Through the use of this document, you appoint a collection agency to collect the delinquent account. This method of collection differs slightly from the actual assignment of the account for collection, in that the appointment of the agent for collection is only for a limited period of time and the fee which the collection agent earns is entirely dependent upon their ability to actually collect the money which is owed to you. This is known as a *contingent fee arrangement*. The collection agent may act on your behalf in attempting to collect the account, but does not have actual ownership of the account. You may limit the actions that the agent takes or spell out specific steps you wish taken with the special instructions. Generally, the payments will continue to be made to your company.

Notice of Appointment of Collection Agent: This form should be used in conjunction with the above form. While the appointment form above is used between your business and the collection service, this form should be used to notify the delinquent account of the appointment of the collection agent for their account. It instructs the customer to make payments to your company or contact the collection agent.

Notice of Disputed Account: This form should be used by you if you have received a statement with which you disagree. If you feel that the statement is in error, spell out your reasoning in the space provided and send this form to the creditor.

Offer to Settle Disputed Account: This form is also intended to be used by your company if you dispute a statement sent to you by others. Through the use of this form, you can offer a compromise settlement on the account. A check in the amount of your compromised settlement can safely be sent with this offer, since, by the terms of the offer, cashing the check will be acceptance of the offer to compromise. Many companies will jump at the cash in hand and agree to concede the remaining balance. This document should only be used if there is an actual dispute regarding the amount owed.

Agreement to Settle Disputed Account: This is a formal version of the above letter agreement. This form may be used to spell out the terms of the compromise settlement more clearly. It should be used by your company if you have received an informal settlement offer from another party to settle an account.

Notice of Dishonored Check: This document should be sent to anyone whose bad check has been returned to you from a bank. It is generally a good idea to attempt to have the check cleared twice before beginning the collection process with this letter. This provides time for last-minute deposits to clear and will often allow the check to clear. This document gives notice to the person of the dishonored check, notifies them of your policy and charges regarding service charges for bad checks, and provides a time limit for clearing up the bad check prior to legal action. Once the check has been paid, return the original check to the debtor.

Stop Payment on Check Order: This form is intended to be provided to a bank or similar financial institution to confirm a telephone stop-payment request. This form provides the institution with written confirmation of the oral request to stop payment on a check.

Request for Payment

Date: _____ , 20 _____

To: _____

RE: Payment of Your Account

Dear _____ :

Regarding your loan, please be advised that we show the following outstanding balance on our books:

Invoice # _____ Date _____ Amount $ _____
Invoice # _____ Date _____ Amount $ _____
Interest on account at _____ percent   Amount $ _____
Late charges   Amount $ _____
Less credits and payments   Amount $ _____

TOTAL BALANCE DUE   AMOUNT $ _____

Please be advised that we have not yet received payment on this outstanding balance. We are certain that this is merely an oversight and would ask that you please send the payment now. Please disregard this notice if full payment has been forwarded to us.

Thank you for your immediate attention to this matter.

Very truly,

_____
Signature

_____
Printed Name

Second Request for Payment

Date: _____ , 20 _____

To: _____

RE: Payment of Your Account

Dear _____ :

Regarding your account, please be advised that we continue to show the following outstanding balance on our books:

Invoice # _____ Date _____ Amount $ _____
Invoice # _____ Date _____ Amount $ _____
Interest on account at _____ percent   Amount $ _____
Late charges   Amount $ _____
Less credits and payments   Amount $ _____

TOTAL BALANCE DUE   AMOUNT $ _____

Please be advised that since our last request for payment dated _____ , 20 _____ , we have still not yet received payment on this outstanding balance. We must request that you please send the payment immediately. Please disregard this notice if full payment has been forwarded to us.

Thank you for your immediate attention to this matter.

Very truly,

_____
Signature

_____
Printed Name

Final Demand for Payment

Date: _____ , 20 _____

To:_____

RE: Payment of Your Account

Dear _____ :

Regarding your delinquent account in the amount of $ _____ , we have requested payment on this account several times without success.

THIS IS YOUR FINAL NOTICE.

Please be advised that unless we receive payment in full on this account in this office within ten (10) days of the date of this letter, we will immediately turn this account over to our attorneys for collection proceedings against you without further notice.

These proceedings will include claims for pre-judgment interest on your account and all legal and court-related costs in connection with collection of this past-due account and will substantially increase the amount that you owe us. Collection proceedings may also have an adverse effect on your credit rating.

We regret the necessity for this action and urge you to clear up this account delinquency immediately. If full payment has been sent, please disregard this notice.

Thank you for your immediate attention to this serious matter.

Very truly,

_____
Signature

_____
Printed Name

Assignment of Account for Collection

This assignment of account for collection is made on _____ , 20 _____ , by and between _____ , assignor, of

_____ ,
City of _____ , State of _____ , and

_____ , assignee, of

_____ ,
City of _____ , State of _____ . It is regarding the account receivable due to the assignor from a customer of the assignor, known as

_____ , customer, of

_____ ,
City of _____ , State of _____ .

As of this date, the account receivable balance is $ _____ .

For valuable consideration, the parties agree as follows:

1. The assignee agrees to pay to the assignor on this day the sum of $ _____ , in return for which the assignor assigns all rights, title, and interest in this account receivable to the assignee for collection.

2. Assignor shall indemnify and hold harmless the assignee from any and all claims arising from the account receivable or the underlying contract between the assignor and the customer. Assignor agrees to furnish the assignee all information required by the assignee in its collection efforts. Assignor agrees to notify the customer of this assignment and to pay to the assignee any payments on this account which are received from the customer after this date.

Dated _____ , 20 _____

_____
Signature of Assignor

_____
Printed Name of Assignor

_____
Signature of Assignee

_____
Printed Name of Assignee

Notice of Assignment of Account for Collection

Date: _____ , 20 _____

To: _____

RE: Assignment of Account for Collection

Dear _____ :

Please be advised that as of _____ , 20 _____ , the following account
receivable balance has been assigned for collection to the firm of
_____ , of
_____ ,
City of _____ , State of _____ .

Invoice Number	Date	Amount
_____	_____	$ _____
_____	_____	$ _____
_____	_____	$ _____
_____	_____	$ _____
_____	_____	$ _____

Interest on account at _____ % $ _____
Late charges $ _____
Less credits and payments $ _____

TOTAL BALANCE DUE $ _____

Please contact the above firm regarding all future payments on this account.

Very truly,

_____   _____
Signature   Printed Name

Appointment of Collection Agent

This agreement for the appointment of collection agent is made on _____ , 20 _____ , by and between _____ , seller, of _____ , City of _____ , State of _____ , and _____ , agent, of

City of _____ , State of _____ . It is regarding the account receivable due to the seller from a customer of the seller, known as _____ , customer, of

City of _____ , State of _____ .

As of this date, the account receivable balance is $ _____ .

For valuable consideration, the parties agree as follows:

1. Seller appoints agent to collect this account receivable from customer on behalf of seller. Agent will be entitled to a contingent fee of _____ % (_____ percent) of whatever amount of the account receivable is collected by agent, payable to the agent upon receipt of the collected amounts. Agent is also subject to the following special instructions:

2. Seller shall indemnify and hold harmless the agent from any and all claims arising from the account receivable or the underlying contract between the seller and the customer. Agent shall indemnify and hold harmless the seller from any and all claims arising from the agent's collection efforts. Seller agrees to furnish the agent all information required by the agent in its collection efforts. Seller agrees to notify the customer of this appointment.

Dated _____ , 20 _____

_____
Signature of Seller

_____
Signature of Agent

_____
Printed Name of Seller

_____
Printed Name of Agent

Notice of Appointment of Collection Agent

Date: _____ , 20 _____

To: _____

RE: Appointment of Collection Agent

Dear _____ :

Please be advised that as of _____ , 20 _____ , the firm of
_____ , of
_____ ,
City of _____ , State of _____ , has been appointed as
agent for collection of the following account receivable balance:

Invoice Number	Date	Amount
_____	_____	$ _____
_____	_____	$ _____
_____	_____	$ _____
_____	_____	$ _____
_____		

Interest on account at _____ % $ _____
Late charges   Amount $ _____
Less credits and payments   Amount $ _____

TOTAL BALANCE DUE   AMOUNT $ _____

You may continue to make your payments to our company or you may make further payments
to the collection agent. Thank you.

Very truly,

_____   _____
Signature   Printed Name

Notice of Disputed Account

Date: _____ , 20 _____

To:_____

RE: Disputed Account

Dear _____ :

We are in receipt of your statement of our account dated _____ , 20 _____ , indicating a balance due you of $ _____ .

We dispute this amount due for the following reasons:

Please contact us immediately to discuss the adjustment of our account.

Very truly,

_____
Signature

_____
Printed Name

Offer to Settle Disputed Account

Date: _____ , 20 _____

To: _____

RE: Disputed Account

Dear _____ :

We are in receipt of your statement of our account dated _____ , 20 _____ , indicating a balance due you of $ _____ .

As noted in our previous letter dated _____ , 20 _____ , we dispute this amount due for the following reasons:

Without admitting any liability on this account, but as an offer to compromise the amount due, we offer to settle this account in full by our payment to you of $ _____ .

Our check # _____ in that amount is enclosed. Your deposit of that check shall confirm your acceptance of our offer to settle this account and shall discharge the entire balance claimed.

Very truly,

_____   _____
Signature   Printed Name

Agreement to Settle Disputed Account

This agreement to settle disputed account is made on _____, 20 _____, by and between _____, seller, of _____, City of _____, State of _____, and _____, customer, of _____, City of _____, State of _____, regarding a disputed account payable dated _____, 20 _____, in the amount of $ _____, based on the following invoices:

Invoice Number	Date	Amount
_____	_____	$ _____
_____	_____	$ _____
_____	_____	$ _____
_____	_____	$ _____

For valuable consideration, the parties agree as follows:

1. The seller will accept a lesser payment of $ _____, in full settlement of the claim on this account.

2. If the customer does not pay the seller this lesser payment within ten (10) days of receipt of a signed original copy of this agreement, the seller may sue the customer for the full amount of the disputed account payable.

3. If the customer pays the lesser payment within the time allowed for payment, both parties mutually release each other from any and all claims or rights to sue each other arising from their dispute over payment of this account payable.

4. This agreement binds and benefits both parties and any successors.

Dated _____, 20 _____

_____
Signature of Seller

_____
Signature of Customer

_____
Printed Name of Seller

_____
Printed Name of Customer

Notice of Dishonored Check

Date: _____ , 20 _____

To: _____

RE: Dishonored Check

Dear _____ :

Please be advised that payment on your check # _____ , dated _____ , 20 _____ , in the amount of $ _____ , has been refused by your bank, _____ , of _____ , City of _____ , State of _____ . We have verified with your bank that there are insufficient funds to pay the check.

Therefore, we request that you immediately replace this check with cash or a certified check for the amount of the bad check and an additional $ _____ as our service charge.

Unless we receive such payment within ten (10) days from the date of this letter, or such further time as may be allowed by state law, we will immediately commence appropriate legal action for recovery of our funds. Please be advised that such legal proceedings may substantially increase the amount owed to us and may include prejudgment interest and legal and court costs.

Upon receipt of payment, we will return your check to you. Thank you for your prompt response to this serious matter.

Very truly,

_____   _____
Signature   Printed Name

Stop Payment on Check Order

Date: _____ , 20 _____

To:_____

RE: Stop Payment on Check

Dear _____ :

Pursuant to our telephone conversation of _____ , 20 _____ ,
please stop payment on the following check:

Account name _____

Account # _____

Check # _____

Check date _____

Check amount _____

Payable to _____

Thank you for your immediate attention to this matter.

Very truly,

_____
Signature

_____
Printed Name

CHAPTER 19
Miscellaneous Business Documents

Included in this chapter are various documents that may be used in a variety of circumstances. These documents range from a form for making sworn statements to an indemnity agreement that may be used by a party to accept responsibility for any claims or liability that may arise in a transaction. The forms that are included and the information necessary to prepare them are as follows:

Instructions

Affidavit: This form is a basic form for an affidavit. An *affidavit* is a legal document with which a person can make a sworn statement regarding anything. It is essentially testimony under oath by the person making the affidavit. An affidavit may be used to document an aspect of a business transaction. It can be used for verification purposes. It may also be used as a supplement to a lawsuit, as the form provided is made under penalty of perjury.

The information necessary to prepare the basic affidavit is the name and address of the person making the affidavit and a written recital of the statement that the person is affirming. This form should be notarized as the statement is being made under oath and under penalty of perjury. If the person making the affirmed statement is acting in other than an individual capacity (as the director of a corporation, for example), substitute the appropriate signature and acknowledgment forms from Chapter 4.

Indemnity Agreement: This form may be used as a general supplement to certain business transactions. With this form, one party to a transaction agrees to indemnify and hold the other party harmless. What this means is that the party doing the indemnifying (the *indemnifier*) will pay for and defend against any legal claims or liabilities against the person being indemnified (the *indemnitee*) that may arise in the future based on the transaction. Unfortunately, there are no other English words that carry the precise meaning necessary to name the parties in this context.

The indemnifier, by this agreement, agrees to defend against any claims or liabilities arising from the transaction. The indemnitee agrees to promptly notify the indemnifier of any such claims. If the indemnifier does not pay for or defend against such claims, the indemnitee has the right to do so and demand reimbursement from the indemnifier.

To prepare this form, complete the following information: the names and addresses of the parties involved, a complete description of the transaction being indemnified, and the name of the state whose laws will govern the agreement.

Waiver and Assumption of Risk: This form may be used in situations in which a customer is either using a business's facilities, receiving instruction, renting equipment, or participating in activities sponsored by a business. If there is any possibility of injury or harm, this form provides a method for the customer to assume the risk of the activity and waive any right to file a claim against the business.

By this form, a customer agrees that he or she has been informed of and understands the risks involved, and that he or she agrees to abide by any safety rules and to act in a non-negligent manner while using the facility or item or while participating in the instruction or activity.

The items needed to fill in this document are the names and addresses of the customer and the owner, the type of activity or instruction, and the age of the customer.

Contract Exhibit: This form may be used with any contract. It provides a simple method for attaching other documents to the contract and having them be considered a legal part of the contract. If you have documents, letters, forms, etc. that you feel are necessary to have as a part of a contract, use this simple form. The space after "Exhibit" in the title and first line of this document is for placing a letter to describe this exhibit (for example, Exhibit A). In the space provided, describe clearly the particular contract to which the exhibit is to be attached (for example, the Contract dated June 1, 2004, between Smith Upholstery Company of 111 Main St., Uptown, NY and Johnson Chair Company of 222 Broadway Ave., Los Angeles, CA).

Assignment and Transfer of Copyright: This particular form should be used to transfer the copyright of a particular piece of creative work to another person or entity. It provides that the copyright owner sells the copyright to a buyer and transfer all rights and interest to that copyright to the new buyer. This includes the rights to make any copies of a creative work, the right to any royalties, and the right to sell or lease any of the worldwide rights to make copies of the work. In order to complete this form, fill in the date, names, and addresses of the copyright owner and buyer, the title of the creative work, and a description of such. In addition, the price paid for the creative work should be included. Please note that this form must be notarized.

Request for Reprint Permission: This form is for use in requesting the right to reprint text or photographs from another source, generally the publisher of the text or illustration. To complete this form, include the date, the title of the publication in which the material appears, and the author or creator of the material. For text, include the page and line numbers of the material, the first and last words to be reprinted, and a total word count. For illustrations or photos, list the page numbers and a description and total number of the illustrations to be reprinted. Also include the manner of the reprinting desired. Finally, you must include the name of the copyright owner and the date of the copyright for use on the credit line and copyright notice in the reprint.

Reprint Permission: This form is for use in granting the right to reprint text or photographs from another source. This form will be used if you are the publisher or creator of the text or illustration. To complete this form, include the date, the name and address of the person seeking permission, the title of the publication in which the material appears, and the name of the author or creator of the material. For text, include the page and line numbers of the material, the first and last words to be reprinted, and a total word count. For illustrations or photos, list the page numbers and a description and total number of the illustrations to be reprinted. Also include the manner of the reprinting desired. Finally, you must include the name of the copyright owner and the date of the copyright for use on the credit line and copyright notice in the reprint.

Model's Photographic Release: This release is for use if photographs of a model are to be used for any type of commercial or advertising use. It grants the holder of the release the right to use the photos in any commercial manner without prior approval of the model. To complete this form, include the date, the amount paid to the model, the name and address of the person given permission to use the photos, the name and address of the photographer, and the date the photos were taken. The name and address of the model should also be included.

Affidavit

I,_____ ,
being of legal age, make the following statements and declare that, on my own personal
knowledge, they are true:

Signed under the penalty of perjury on _____ , 20 _____ .

_____
Signature

_____
Printed Name

State of _____
County of _____

On _____ , 20 _____ , _____ personally
came before me and, being duly sworn, did state that he or she is the person described in the
above document and that he or she signed the above document in my presence.

_____
Signature of Notary Public

Notary Public, In and for the County of _____
State of _____

My commission expires: _____   Notary Seal

Indemnity Agreement

This indemnity agreement is made on _____ , 20 _____ , between
_____ , indemnifier, of
_____ ,
City of _____ , State of _____ , and
_____ , indemnitee, of
_____ ,
City of _____ , State of _____ .

For valuable consideration, the parties agree as follows:

1. The indemnifier agrees to indemnify and hold the indemnitee harmless from any claim or liability arising from the following activity:

2. In the event of any claim or asserted liability against the indemnitee arising from the above activity, the indemnitee agrees to provide the indemnifier with prompt written notice. Upon notice, the indemnifier agrees to defend and save the indemnitee harmless from any loss or liability. In the event the indemnifier fails to indemnify the indemnitee, the indemnitee has the right to defend or settle any claim on their own behalf and be fully reimbursed by the indemnifier for all costs and expenses of such defense or settlement.

3. No modification of this agreement will be effective unless it is in writing and is signed by both parties. This agreement binds and benefits both parties and any successors. This document, including any attachments, is the entire agreement between the parties. This agreement is governed by the laws of the State of _____ .

Dated _____ , 20 _____

_____   _____
Signature of Indemnifier   Signature of Indemnitee

_____   _____
Printed Name of Indemnifer   Printed Name of Indemnitee

Waiver and Assumption of Risk

I, _____ , customer, of

_____ ,
City of _____ , State of _____ , voluntarily sign this waiver
and assumption of risk in favor of

_____ , owner, of

_____ ,
City of _____ , State of _____ , in consideration for the
opportunity to use the owner's facilities and/or the opportunity to receive instruction from
the owner or the owner's employees, and/or to engage in the activities sponsored by the
owner, as follows:

I understand that there are certain risks and dangers associated with the activity and use
of the facilities and that these risks have been fully explained to me. I fully understand the
danger involved.

I fully assume the risks involved as acceptable to me and I agree to use my best judgment in
undertaking these activities and follow all safety instructions.

I waive and release the owner from any claim for personal injury, property damage, or death
that may arise from my use of the facilities or from my participation in the activities or instruction.

I am a competent adult, aged _____ , and I assume these risks of my own
free will.

Dated _____ , 20 _____

_____   _____
Signature of Customer   Printed Name of Customer

Contract Exhibit _____

This Contract Exhibit _____ is attached and made part of the following contract:

Assignment and Transfer of Copyright

This assignment and transfer of copyright is made on _____ , 20 _____ ,
by _____ , owner, of
_____ ,
City of _____ , State of _____ , to
_____ , buyer, of
_____ ,
City of _____ , State of _____ .

The owner is the sole owner of the full and exclusive copyright of a work titled
_____ , described as:

a copy of which is attached and is considered a part of this document. The buyer desires to buy the entire interest of the owner in the work.

In consideration of $ _____ , for which the owner acknowledges receipt, the owner assigns and transfers to the buyer and the buyer's heirs, assigns, and representatives, all of the owner's rights and interest in the work and its copyright throughout the world, including the right to any renewals or extensions of the copyright. The owner has signed this document on the date stated above.

_____
Signature of Copyright Owner   Printed Name of Copyright Owner

State of _____
County of _____

On _____ , 20 _____ , _____ personally came before me and, being duly sworn, did state that he or she is the person described in the above document and that he or she signed the above document in my presence.

_____
Signature of Notary Public

Notary Public, In and for the County of _____
State of _____

My commission expires: _____ , 20 _____   Notary Seal

Request for Reprint Permission

Date: _____ , 20 _____

To: _____

RE: Reprint Permission

Dear _____ :

We request permission for the non-exclusive right to reprint the following material:

From: _____
By: _____

Textual material

From page _____ , line _____ , through page _____ , line _____ ,
beginning with the words " _____ " and ending with the words
" _____ ," and consisting of a total of _____ words.

Illustration(s)

On page _____ , described as:

and consisting of _____ illustration(s)/photograph(s).

We intend to reprint the material in the following manner:

The following credit line and copyright notice will accompany the use of this material:

"Used by permission of _____ ,
Copyright _____ "

Thank you very much.

_____   _____
Signature   Printed Name

Reprint Permission

Date: _____ , 20 _____

To: _____

RE: Reprint Permission

Dear _____ :

Please be advised that permission is granted to:

_____ , of

_____ ,

City of _____ , State of _____ , for non-exclusive one-time reprint rights of the following material:

From: _____
By: _____

From: _____
By: _____

Textual material

From page _____ , line _____ , through page _____ , line _____ , beginning with the words " _____ " and ending with the words " _____ ," and consisting of a total of _____ words.

From page _____ , line _____ , through page _____ , line _____ , beginning with the words " _____ " and ending with the words " _____ ," and consisting of a total of _____ words.

Illustration(s)

On page _____ , described as:

On page _____ , described as:

and consisting of _____ illustration(s)/photograph(s).

Permission is granted to reprint the above material in the following manner:

The following credit line and copyright notice must accompany the use of this material:

"Used by permission of _____ ,
Copyright _____ "

Permission is granted on _____ , 20 _____ .

Very truly,

_____   _____
Signature of Copyright Owner   Printed Name of Copyright Owner

Model's Photographic Release

Date: _____ , 20 _____

For payment received in the amount of $ _____ , and other valuable consideration, permission is granted to

_____ , of

_____ ,
City of _____ , State of _____ , for exclusive world rights, including copyright, and use of any photographs containing my image which were taken by

_____ , of

_____ ,
City of _____ , State of _____ , on
_____ , 20 _____ .

In addition, I also grant _____ , of

_____ ,
City of _____ , State of _____ all rights for subsidiary use, promotional use, future revisions, and future editions of the same.

I waive any right to inspect or approve final use of such photographs and I waive any right to file any legal actions, including libel or invasion of privacy, based on any use of the photographs under this release.

I am over 21 and understand the content of this document.

Permission is granted on _____ , 20 _____ .

_____   _____
Signature of Model   Printed Name of Model

_____   _____
Address of Model   City and State of Model

Index

✯ Nova Publishing Company ✯
Small Business and Consumer Legal Books and Software

Law Made Simple Series
Basic Wills Simplified
ISBN 0-935755-90-X	Book only	$22.95
ISBN 0-935755-89-6	Book w/Forms-on-CD	$28.95

Divorce Agreements Simplified
ISBN 0-935755-87-X	Book only	$24.95
ISBN 0-935755-86-1	Book w/Forms-on-CD	$29.95

Living Trusts Simplified
ISBN 0-935755-53-5	Book only	$22.95
ISBN 0-935755-51-9	Book w/Forms-on-CD	$28.95

Living Wills Simplified
ISBN 0-935755-52-7	Book only	$22.95
ISBN 0-935755-50-0	Book w/Forms-on-CD	$28.95

Personal Bankruptcy Simplified (3rd Edition)
ISBN 1-892949-01-6	Book only	$22.95
ISBN 1-892949-02-4	Book w/Forms-on-CD	$28.95

Personal Legal Forms Simplified (3rd Edition)
ISBN 0-935755-97-7	Book w/Forms-on-CD	$28.95

Small Business Made Simple Series
Corporation: Small Business Start-up Kit (2nd Edition)
ISBN 1-892949-06-7	Book w/Forms-on-CD	$29.95

The Complete Book of Small Business Management Forms
ISBN 0-935755-56-X	Book w/Forms-on-CD	$24.95

Limited Liability Company: Small Business Start-up Kit (2nd Edition)
ISBN 1-892949-04-0	Book w/Forms-on-CD	$29.95

Partnerships: Small Business Start-up Kit
ISBN 0-935755-75-6	Book w/Forms-on-CD	$24.95

S-Corporation: Small Business Start-up Kit (2nd Edition)
ISBN 1-892949-05-9	Book w/Forms-on-CD	$29.95

Small Business Accounting Simplified (3rd Edition)
ISBN 0-935755-91-8	Book only	$22.95

Small Business Bookkeeping Systems Simplified
ISBN 0-935755-74-8	Book only	$14.95

Small Business Legal Forms Simplified (4th Edition)
ISBN 0-935755-98-5	Book w/Forms-on-CD	$29.95

Small Business Payroll Systems Simplified
ISBN 0-935755-55-1	Book only	$14.95

Sole Proprietorship: Small Business Start-up Kit
ISBN 0-935755-79-9	Book w/Forms-on-CD	$24.95

Legal Self-Help Series
Divorce Yourself: The National No-Fault Divorce Kit (5th Edition)
ISBN 0-935755-93-4	Book only	$24.95
ISBN 0-935755-94-2	Book w/Forms-on-CD	$34.95

Incorporate Now!: The National Corporation Kit (4th Edition)
ISBN 1-892949-00-8	Book w/Forms-on-CD	$29.95

Prepare Your Own Will: The National Will Kit (5th Edition)
ISBN 0-935755-72-1	Book only	$17.95
ISBN 0-935755-73-X	Book w/Forms-on-CD	$27.95

National Legal Kits
Simplified Bankruptcy Kit
ISBN 0-935755-83-7	Book only	$17.95

Simplified Divorce Kit
ISBN 0-935755-81-0	Book only	$19.95

Simplified Will Kit
ISBN 0-935755-96-9	Book only	$16.95

✯ Ordering Information ✯

Distributed by:
National Book Network
4501 Forbes Blvd. Suite 200
Lanham MD 20706

Shipping: $4.50 for first & $.75 for each additional
Phone orders with Visa/MC: (800) 462-6420
Fax orders with Visa/MC: (800) 338-4550
Internet: www.novapublishing.com